Wild
SUGAR

Wild SUGAR

Seasonal
Sweet Treats
Inspired
by the
Mountain
West

LINDSEY JOHNSON Lady in the Wild West
WITH CHASE REYNOLDS EWALD

Gibbs Smith

FIRST EDITION
28 27 26 25 24   5 4 3 2 1

Text © 2024 Lindsey Johnson and Chase Reynolds Ewald
Photographs © 2024 Lindsey Johnson, except as listed below

PHOTO CREDITS
Jay Goodrich Photography: pages 50, 52–53, 134–135, 145
Sylvie Gil: page 8
Lindley Rust: pages 82, 100, 101, 160, 190
Julie Jay Photos: page 174
Woodgrain art from Northern Owl/Shutterstock.com
Floral art from sarodigiart/Shutterstock.com

PUBLISHED BY
Gibbs Smith
P.O. Box 667
Layton, Utah 84041

1.800.835.4993 orders
www.gibbs-smith.com

DESIGNER: Eva Spring
ART DIRECTOR: Ryan Thomann
EDITOR: Michelle Branson
PRODUCTION DESIGNER: Renee Bond

Printed and bound in China
Gibbs Smith books are printed on either recycled, 100% post-consumer
waste, FSC-certified papers or on paper produced from sustainable PEFC-
certified forest/controlled wood source. Learn more at www.pefc.org.

Library of Congress Control Number: 2023941873
ISBN: 978-1-4236-6361-4

To my bear cubs,
Hatton, Killian, and Soren.
You are the reason
my life is so sweet.

CONTENTS

Fall

Winter

FOREWORD

THE DEFINITION OF ART IS "the expression or application of human creative skill and imagination." Lindsey Johnson is an artist at the top of her game. As an actress, I am in awe of and inspired by baking as an art form.

Baking and acting have a lot in common. Baking and acting are about transformation, about bringing memories to life. They both require you to live completely and fully in the present moment, allowing your senses to take center stage and your mind to stay quiet. Baking is creative, a blank canvas of butter, sugar, and flour inspiring infinite possibilities, much like an actress explores new possibilities in her performance take after take.

I first met Lindsey when she created our beautiful wedding cake and dessert bar for our wedding. Having grown up watching Westerns with my father, an obsession with horses and the Wild West has always been part of my DNA. I knew I wanted my wedding in the West, full of nature, wildflowers, mountainous landscapes, a perfume of manure, and beautiful horses as our guests of honor. When we accidentally stumbled upon Moose Creek Ranch on a trip to Jackson Hole, Wyoming, in 2017, we knew it was where we must celebrate our love. It checked every box.

It was very important to both of us that the wedding be authentic to who we are as people. We explained to Lindsey our love of animals and the outdoors. Especially our love of the 50,000 bees we kept in the backyard who dined daily on our lavender bushes. She immediately suggested my favorite dessert, a honey-lavender cake using the honey from our bees and the lavender from our garden. I have *dreams* about this cake. It is still discussed at family gatherings as one of the best, and definitely the most *delicious*, parts of our wedding.

Lindsey inspired a lifelong love of baking in me. Though my creations have a VERY long way to go in looking as beautiful as hers, I appreciate the art of baking because I never need to depend on anyone but myself. There's a beginning, a middle, and an end. Baking is a beautiful way to say thank you, I'm sorry, and I love you. Even if your creations don't look perfect, they can still taste delicious—the only measure of baking "success" in my book. And I can guarantee you Lindsey's recipes taste as delicious as they look.

I hope baking your way through this book is as creative and inspiring for you as it was for me. Thank you, Lindsey, for inspiring me so deeply, and for giving Michael and our loved ones memories of a lifetime through your sweet creations!

—*Beth Behrs*

INTRODUCTION

Be the Buffalo

JOHN MUIR SAID, "The mountains are calling and I must go."

I was born and raised in the charming coastal town of San Clemente, California. It's known for having the best climate in the world, grooming surf champs, and perfecting irresistible fish tacos. I love my hometown and my beach-girl roots, but as was the case for John Muir, the mountains were calling. And the calls grew louder every day.

In the spring of 2016, my husband and I took a giant risk. We left our cozy beach town, our jobs, and our families and moved our three boys to Jackson, Wyoming, a place we'd never spent time in. We had no connections and, honestly, not much of a plan. What an adventure, we thought! Raising our boys in the great wide open—the Wild West—just as we'd always dreamed. As long as we were together, everything would work out just fine.

Well . . . we should have made a plan. That first year in Jackson turned out to be the most challenging year of my life.

To make ends meet, my husband traveled back to California for work; sometimes he'd be gone for weeks at a time. With my youngest son barely walking, I had my hands full being a full-time mom. I didn't get out much. I hadn't made any new friends. Living just outside of Grand Teton National Park, about twenty-five minutes from town, I felt intimidated by my rustic surroundings. Trading cute sea lions for snarling mountain lions was a big change. I desperately missed my family, my friends, my career, and as time dragged on, myself. I was in this beautiful place, our new home. But I had never felt more lost and lonely. I began to fear we had made a mistake.

When that first winter came around, it was harsh. And I mean, *harsh*. Negative temperatures, icy roads, and snow piling three feet against our windows. Remember that scene in Stephen King's *The Shining* when Jack Nicholson is staring out the window into a blizzard slowly losing his mind? That was me. I wasn't about to become an axe murderer, but I was struggling. My happiest moments were found in hugs from the kids, baking cookies, and well, eating cookies. The days blended together. I was in desperate need of grown-up conversation. I had also gained ten pounds of pure cookie dough.

One snowy winter day, when my husband was away for work, I decided to head to the local library. It was the only place I knew to go where the boys could play with other kids and make friends. The only thing standing in our way was the Mount Everest–size pile of snow blocking the car. I bundled everyone up, headed outside, and relentlessly began attacking the mountain of snow blocking me from civilization. Suddenly, I slipped on a patch of ice. I fell *hard*, flat on my back. It hurt like hell. I said some words I can't repeat and began to cry. I remember thinking to myself, "This is the moment when I die. The snow will cover me and they won't find my body until spring." I lay there, helpless and pathetic, letting the storm of life come down on me. My boys came running over, worried and scared. "Mommy, Mommy, are you okay?!" I looked at their hopeful eyes and knew, for them, I had to be okay. I lifted myself up and kept on shoveling, all the while thinking, "What am I doing here?"

The library was packed with kids and moms escaping the snow. The boys ran off happily to explore. I spotted a fellow mom and went to sit beside her. Maybe I'll make a new friend. Not knowing how to start a conversation, I looked at her hat. It was a buffalo, roaming the plains, with mountains behind it. It gave me a sense of peace. I said to her, "I really like your hat." She turned my way and gave me a warm smile. She said, "You know the story of the buffalo, don't you?" I shook my head no. Then she told me the story.

"The buffalo is the only creature in nature that can sense when a storm is coming. Most animals run, but the buffalo chooses to charge the storm. The buffalo knows that charging the storm, fighting its way through, is its best chance for survival. So, when life feels like a storm, you remember, be the buffalo. Charge your storm."

She smiled again, affectionately touched my knee, and walked away.

Have you ever had a time when you feel like the universe is speaking directly to you? Your perspective flips. You see the big picture. You are awake. I have. That was my big bang moment.

My storm was here. Everything in my body wanted to run. I wanted to run back *home*, to my safe, familiar, easy life. But the buffalo wouldn't run. The buffalo would charge. I wanted to be the buffalo. And so I was.

I began to ask myself, aside from being a wife and mom, who am I? What do I want? What am I good at? Days went by, many cookies were eaten, and ideas came and went. I still felt like I hadn't found my place in this Wild West town. What I did know, however, is I'm happiest when I'm creating. When I'm being artistic. And evidently, when I'm baking cookies. But what could I do with that . . . ? Lightbulb!

Since I was little, baking cookies, pies, and cakes has brought me joy. I loved adding artistic details, using gourmet ingredients, and styling them beautifully. Even more, I loved sharing my creations with others, bringing them joy, too. Suddenly, everything made sense. By mixing baking with art, I can be creative in a way I'd never considered before. Letting the beauty of the mountains and the Wild West inspire me, I can create edible art.

So I began. I started small, with birthday cakes and baby showers, and soon grew to catering gorgeous weddings under the Teton Mountains. Slowly, but surely, I came back to life. Wyoming became home. I became someone new. I became a buffalo.

Sometimes we need to get lost to be found. Sometimes we need to break to rebuild. Sometimes the most beautiful view comes after a storm. And sometimes, the universe has a plan for us.

—*Lindsey Johnson*

BAKING BASICS

Picasso said, "Learn the rules like a pro, so you can break them like an artist." As with any craft, we begin with the basics.

Bring it to room temperature

If a recipe calls for room-temperature ingredients, it's for good reason. Think of your cake as a party and your ingredients as the guests. To create a light and fluffy texture, it's all about blending in at the party. Cold ingredients, just like cold party guests, don't blend. However, the term room temperature can be tricky. For example, my room temperature during a Wyoming winter is different from a room temperature in Florida. My general rule is to set the chilled ingredients out roughly an hour before I start mixing.

Measuring matters

The ingredient most over measured is flour, which can result in a dry and dense cake. Flour sitting in a bag or canister gets packed in. Before measuring, use a spoon to stir and lighten the flour. Then use the spoon to scoop the flour into your measuring cup, scraping any overfill off with your finger or rubber spatula. You can also use a scale for more precise measurements, but I'll be honest, I've never weighed ingredients. The old-school method has worked fine for me.

Measuring for dry ingredients and wet ingredients is not the same. For wet ingredients use liquid measuring cups. Keep the cup on a flat surface and check the measurement at eye level.

It doesn't matter how many cakes I've made, I can be forgetful, especially when it comes to leaveners. A good practice is to measure all the ingredients ahead of time so you don't miss a thing.

Prep work is key

There is nothing worse than a cake that sticks to the pan. Always wipe your cake pan interiors evenly with a grease (butter, shortening, or nonstick spray) and a dusting of flour. For chocolate cakes I use cocoa powder instead of flour. For extra measure, I add parchment paper to the bottom of the pans. Using the cake pan as a size guide, trace the bottom and cut out the shape. After greasing and flouring, fit the parchment circle into the bottom of the pan. This method works for brownies and bars as well. For cupcake pans I use paper liners, but if you're not using liners I recommend greasing and flouring. For cookies, line the baking sheets with parchment paper or silicone baking mats.

I highly recommend aluminum pans for their ability to conduct heat evenly. This ensures an even rise for your cakes, cupcakes, and cookies. They're very lightweight, inexpensive, and last forever. My favorite brands are Nordic Ware and Fat Daddio's.

Mix it up

My most valuable piece of advice through the mixing process is: follow the steps. Take the time needed to cream your butter and sugar until it's light and fluffy. Let the sugar beat up that butter and incorporate those happy air bubbles. Add your eggs, one at a time, so each is properly blended into the batter. Stop every now and then to scrape down the bowl. Be patient when alternating your wet ingredients with your dry ingredients. These steps may seem tedious, but the end result will be worth it. Then toward the end, know when to stop. Overmixing will counteract all the work you did and result in a dry and dense cake.

It's time to bake

Begin preheating the oven about 30 minutes before you're ready to bake. All ovens are different. Because of this, my baking times are more like suggestions. It's worth the trial and error to get to know your oven—for example, where any hot spots may be and if your temperature is off. An oven thermometer is a very handy tool to help tackle these questions.

Aside from the timer going off, there are more reliable ways to check if a cake or cupcakes are fully baked. The toothpick method is most common. Insert a toothpick into the center of the cake and if it comes out clean or with a few crumbs, your cake is done. I like to use what I call the "spring back" method. I lightly press on the center of the cake and if it springs back against my hand, it's fully baked. Another sign is when the cake begins to pull away from the side of the pan. To prevent overbaking, start checking your cake a few minutes before the time suggests.

Cool down

All baked goods continue to bake slightly after you remove them from the oven. We want this, but in the right amount. If you let a baked good sit in its pan for too long it will become soggy. If you remove it too soon you risk it falling apart. For cakes and cupcakes, let them cool for 10 minutes in their pans on a wire rack, then transfer them from their pans to a wire rack to cool completely. For cookies, let them cool on their baking sheet on a wire rack for 5 to 7 minutes. Then transfer them from their pans to a wire rack to cool completely. For brownies and bars, let them cool for 30 minutes in their pans on a wire rack. Then transfer them from their pans to a wire rack to cool completely.

Storing

Room temperature becomes our friend once again. Always let your baked goods cool to room temperature before storing. Store cupcakes, cookies, and bars in airtight containers. For cakes, level the domed tops (see prepare the cake layers, below) and double wrap them tightly in plastic wrap. If you're planning to stack and decorate the same or next day, keep them at room temperature. Well-wrapped cakes and desserts can be frozen for up to 2 months. Let them defrost overnight in the refrigerator then sit at room temperature for an hour before serving.

IT'S ALL ABOUT THE CAKE

Making swoon-worthy cakes begins with stacking, filling, and the crumb coat. A crumb coat is a thin layer of buttercream that covers the exterior of the cake and locks in crumbs and moisture. Consider the crumb coat to be the primer for the beautiful painting you're about to create. Little steps in the beginning lead to grand and beautiful results in the end.

Prepare the cake layers

As cakes rise in the oven, often the surface becomes uneven and domed. Begin by trimming the domed top from the cake layers to create a level surface. Even if the surface of your cake layers are only slightly uneven, take the time to level them for structural integrity. We don't want the finished cake to resemble the Leaning Tower of Pisa. This can be done with a serrated knife, cutting carefully from one side to the other, or with my favorite tool, a Wilton cake leveler. A cake leveler ensures an even height on the cake layers from side to side. Leveling cake layers is best done when the cakes are at room temperature, before you've wrapped them for storing.

Work with chilled cake layers. Chilled, but not frozen through. Frozen cake layers will expand as they come to room temperature, releasing air bubbles and leading to buttercream bulges later on. Let frozen cake layers defrost in the refrigerator overnight before stacking and layering. The cake layers should feel cold and slightly firm to the touch. Chilled layers will make the buttercream and filling stage much easier, ultimately creating a sturdier cake.

Prepare the cake-building surface

For a clean look, I like to build my cakes on clear acrylic disks, but a cardboard cake board works beautifully. You can also build directly on a cake stand or platter, just make sure it's food safe and can be transferred easily to and from the refrigerator. A surface slightly larger than the cake will make the process easier. Add a dollop of buttercream to the center of your surface to work as a glue to secure the bottom cake layer. This will stop the cake layer from sliding around as you begin to frost.

Prepare the buttercream

Before filling piping bags and applying buttercream to the cake layers, stir the buttercream by hand for 3 minutes with a rubber spatula to press out air bubbles. This ensures a smooth coating for the cake layers. Depending on your altitude (I'm at 6,000 feet in elevation), this may need to be done several times as air tends to collect as buttercream sits. My preferred way to add and spread buttercream evenly is with an offset spatula.

Prepare the filling

All fillings should be at room temperature and at a spreadable consistency, especially caramels and ganaches. If the filling is too cold it will seize the buttercream and pull it up as you spread. If the filling is too warm it will melt the buttercream. Both create an unwanted mess. To prevent fillings from seeping over the sides, using a Wilton piping tip 2A, pipe a buttercream border around the edge of the cake layer. This is known as a buttercream dam, which is exactly what it sounds like. The border works as a dam to hold the filling in and the layers securely together.

Prepare the crumb coat

After you have applied the buttercream, filled, and stacked the layers, firmly press the cake down from the top to release any air that has collected during the process. Hidden air pockets will release as you are decorating, creating the dreaded buttercream bulge. Add a generous mound of buttercream to the top and begin to spread evenly outward, covering the entire top then pushing over the sides. Adding more buttercream if needed, spreading to cover the entire cake. Use a metal cake scraper to scrape off excess buildup of buttercream. Don't worry about being neat, this is just a primer. You should see hints of the cake layers underneath, but the entire cake should have a buttercream coating. Run the metal cake scraper under hot water for one to two minutes and wipe it on a clean towel, then give the cake a final smoothing. The heat will create a seamless primed finish.

Prepare for decorating

Chill the crumb-coated cake for at least 20 minutes before adding the final buttercream coat and decorating.

TOOLS OF THE TRADE

Once you've mastered texture, flavor, stacking, and the crumb coat, the real fun begins with decorating. Cake decorating is an art form. Cakes are a canvas on which ideas can be brought to life. There is no right or wrong way to decorate, but a little knowledge on technique and having the right collection of tools can help you create the look you want. As with any tool, practice makes perfect. You'll discover what works best for you.

Pans and Baking Sheets

I highly recommend aluminum pans for their ability to conduct heat evenly. This ensures an even rise for your cakes, cupcakes, bars, and cookies. They're lightweight, inexpensive, and last forever. My favorite brands are Nordic Ware and Fat Daddio's. For cake pans I suggest starting with 6-inch and 8-inch sizes, as that is what most recipes are designed for. Baking sheets will depend on the size of your oven, but I recommend going as large as possible so your cookies have plenty of room to breathe. Cupcakes pans are standard for 1 dozen.

Offset Spatula

An offset or angled spatula is a cake-maker's best friend. You use this tool to spread buttercream evenly between the cake layers and to frost cupcakes. I recommend having two sizes, a 9-inch for small jobs and a 13-inch for large jobs. A straight-edge spatula is used to apply buttercream to the side of the cake. When selecting spatulas, make sure they have a nice heavy handle and feel good in your hand.

Cake Scrapers

A cake scraper is a flat rectangular disk used to smooth the exterior of the cake. Some scrapers have patterned edges to create a unique stripe or scalloped design. I've learned through fellow cake artists that cake scrapers are a very personal tool. Some artists prefer acrylic while others prefer stainless steel. I have used both and recommend you do as well, however, I am team stainless steel all the way. The reason being, you can heat up a stainless-steel cake scraper with hot water, which creates the ultimate smooth buttercream finish. I recommend a 10-inch scraper so you're not restricted by the height of your cake. You hold the scraper vertically at a 90-degree angle against the cake. Drag the straight edge along the side of the cake to smooth. Wipe off the collected buttercream and continue until smooth.

Rotating Cake Stand

A rotating cake stand is a must for cake decorating. It turns so you don't have to, allowing you to see your cake from every angle. It's especially helpful when crumb coating and for the final coat of buttercream. I would steer clear of plastic versions and invest in a quality metal model. A heavy, sturdy base is crucial, especially for larger cakes, and a nonslip rotating surface will keep your cake in place. I recommend a model by Ateco or Puroma.

Piping Tips

Where do I begin? I have over 100 piping tips and have a creative use for every one. Coming in all shapes and sizes, piping tips can be used for basic layer filling and cupcake swirls, but more artistically for writing, piped borders, ruffles, open stars, and buttercream flowers, petals, and leaves. The possibilities are endless. As a new decorator, I purchased a decorating set from Wilton and have never regretted it. Since then I've built my collection based on what I love creating. For me, that's petal tips for buttercream flowers. I recommend Wilton and Ateco tips. Here is a collection of my personal favorites:

ROUND TIPS are used for writing, dots, small lines, filling cake layers and cookie sandwiches, flower centers, sugar cookie decorating, and cupcake swirls:

- Ateco 809
- Wilton 2A
- Wilton tips 1, 2, 3, 4, 5, 6, 7, 8, 9, and 10

STAR TIPS are used for open and closed star shapes, rosettes, roped borders, succulents, and cupcake swirls:

- Ateco 829
- Ateco 843
- Wilton 1M
- Wilton 4B
- Wilton 2D
- Wilton 32
- Wilton 30
- Wilton 21
- Wilton 18

PETAL TIPS are used for creating flowers, succulents, and leaves:

- Ateco 123
- Ateco 124K
- Ateco 125K
- Ateco 126K
- Wilton 124
- Wilton 123
- Wilton 104
- Wilton 102

LEAF TIPS are used for flower petals, succulents, and leaves:

- Wilton 366
- Wilton 352
- Wilton 70
- Wilton 68
- Wilton 349

Piping Bags

To put your piping tips to use you need piping bags. Piping bags can be clear disposable plastic or a featherweight reusable fabric. Both are useful for different functions. Clear disposable bags are sold in high quantities. They are wonderful for piping details and flowers, especially when using multiple colors. They come in different lengths, 12 inches being the most common and useful. Reusable bags are wonderful when frosting cupcakes and cakes and anytime you're using a larger quantity of buttercream. Reusable bags are typically longer in length, like 16 to 18 inches. I keep both disposable and reusable bags on hand. I also reuse my disposable bags; I clean them with warm soapy water and they're good as new. A helpful tip to fill your piping bags with buttercream is to have a tall drinking glass handy. Place the piping bag, fitted with the tip, inside the glass. Fold the end of the bag around the edge of the glass. This holds the bag in place so it's easier to fill.

Palette Knives

Palette knives are typically used for acrylic painting on canvas and can be found at art and craft supply stores. I use palette knives to "paint" with my buttercream, the same way you would with paint. They create beautiful dimension and texture in leaves and flower petals, landscapes, or whatever your imagination holds. They come in many shapes and sizes. I recommend purchasing a set of 3 or 4 to experiment with. They're inexpensive and long lasting. Of all my artistic tools, palette knives are my favorite.

Food Coloring

LIQUID You can find liquid food coloring in the grocery-store bakery aisle. I use liquid food coloring to tint cake batters and to lightly tint buttercream. It's useful when you need a color to disperse quickly without a lot of mixing; however, I draw the line there. If you need a rich, saturated color, liquid food coloring isn't powerful enough and will change the consistency of what you're coloring.

GELS Food gels are a highly concentrated, thick gel color. A little goes a long way and the color options are endless. The benefit of a gel is that you can achieve an intense color without changing the consistency of what you are coloring. Food gels are also highly versatile. I use food gels to tint buttercream, royal icing, and for painted effects. Water-based food gels can be thinned with water or vodka and used like a watercolor. The water or vodka evaporates and leaves the color behind. My favorite food gels are made by AmeriColor or Chefmaster.

OIL-BASED GELS Oil-based food gels are smooth and silky and create the most intense color saturation for buttercream. Because of their oil base, they also blend well with chocolate or candy melts. I don't recommend thinning oil-based gels for a painted effect because they don't dry. My favorite oil-based gels are made by Colour Mill.

Luster Dusts and Edible Gold

For highlights and a pop of glamour, I absolutely love luster dusts and edible gold. Luster dusts come in gold, rose gold, copper, and silver. They can be applied as a dust for a metallic sheen or thinned down with vodka to make a paint. My favorite brands are Luxe Cake and Roxy & Rich. More costly but well worth it is edible gold leaf. Paper thin and very delicate, you only need a tiny amount to make a statement. I apply gold leaf with a paint brush or press the sheet directly onto the cake. My favorite brand is Slofoodgroup.

Paint Brushes

Having different size food-safe paint brushes on hand is always a good idea. They're great for painted details, adding texture, and applying luster dusts and edible gold. Look for a soft brush so you don't disturb the buttercream you're working on. I especially love tiny thin brushes for detailing.

Cold and Heat

I know it sounds silly to mention cold and heat under tools, but I'd be lost without them. Having a refrigerator handy to chill your cake is crucial when you're decorating. Cake making happens in stages. Chilling between those stages so your buttercream stays firm is imperative. When I'm piping, I take breaks to chill my piping bags because my hands warm up the buttercream. I also use heat in the form of hot water. Running the metal cake scraper, spatula, or palette knife under hot water is the best way to blend colors together and get a smooth buttercream finish.

Sprinkles and Dragees

To enhance birthday and holiday cakes, add sprinkles. They're like edible happiness. I have a drawer in my bakery completely devoted to sprinkles of all shapes, colors, and styles. Sprinkle makers have kicked it up a notch with truly creative sprinkle mixes. My favorite gourmet sprinkle maker is Sprinkle Pop.

DECORATING TECHNIQUES

Decorating cakes and cookies is a craft and an art form, with the ultimate reward . . . you get to eat it!

The purpose of this book is to share delicious home-style baking recipes, but I'd be remiss if I didn't also share some introduction on how to decorate them. I believe all desserts should be beautiful and artistic; that's part of the indulgence. After all, you eat with your eyes first. Beautiful things taste better. While I don't have the space to offer in-depth step-by-step instruction, I can give some insight into my favorite decorating styles and how to approach them. I learned these styles through experimenting. I encourage you to do the same!

The Painted Cookie

A painting technique on royal icing is my favorite way to decorate sugar cookies. It opens the door to a level of detail that could never be achieved with royal icing alone. I add shading, fine lines, antiquing, and watercolor effects. Cookies become fine art, each one completely unique. I begin by icing the cookies in untinted (white) medium-consistency royal icing. This gives me a plain canvas. I let the cookies dry overnight so the royal icing is firm throughout. To paint, I use AmeriColor or Chefmaster food gels. I do not recommend using Colour Mill food gels as they're oil based and don't dry properly. Because the gels are a thick consistency, I dilute them with vodka. Water may be used as well; however, water can oversaturate the cookies, leaving an unsightly texture. Vodka evaporates more quickly than water, leaving no taste and nothing but color behind.

To paint on cookies, use food-safe art brushes in multiple sizes, and mix the food gels on an artist's palette board or in small bowls. Add the vodka to the gels using an eyedropper. It allows for maximum control over how thin the paint will be. The more vodka added, the lighter the color will become. Keep a small bowl of vodka handy to clean the brushes in between uses. Once the colors are mixed and you're ready to paint, dip the brush into the color then immediately dab the brush lightly onto a paper towel to blot off any excess moisture. The brush should be moistened with color, but not dripping. Much like painting with watercolor, it's important to move quickly and swiftly with the base colors. Finer details can be added later.

In this process, the vodka serves as a diluter and cleaner of the color, but it also works as an eraser of color. Because of this you can't add multiple layers of color without taking some color away. But you can use the eraser effect to create white highlights and clean up mistakes. Dip your brush in vodka and wipe over areas where you'd like to remove color.

Let the cookies dry fully before eating or wrapping.

The Painted Cake

Painted cakes tell a story, and a good story is all about the details. Some artistic details can't be created with buttercream alone. For example, a clean fine line of an elk antler or a detail on the fin of a rainbow trout. When I'm decorating cakes, I become very invested in these details. They often make the design. For this, I turn to food gels and paint brushes. I approach a painted cake much like a painted cookie; however, I'm working on a buttercream base rather than a firm royal-icing base. This presents some challenges and is where chilling the cake comes into use. For painting on cakes, I use water-based food gels or oil-based food gels. Oil-based food gels will allow more leverage with color, letting me layer color on, even light colors over dark. Oil-based food gels are especially useful when I want to add a white highlight. But keep in mind they don't dry as well. However, this isn't as much of a problem as it is with cookies, given we don't wrap cakes in cellophane.

‹
THE PAINTED CAKE

Before adding painted details to a cake, the buttercream must be set and firm to the touch. Chill the cake for 20 minutes before beginning. While painting, keep a very light touch with your brush so as to not break the surface of the buttercream. Paint small sections at a time and chill the cake in between so the buttercream remains firm while you're working.

The Palette Knife Cake

Painting a cake with a palette knife adds dimension, texture, and character. It's a free-form style, purely artistic and rustic. It's not about being perfect, it's about being expressive. This style works well with landscapes; think of the rough edges of Van Gogh's work, or floral designs, much like Monet, or my personal favorite, wildlife. Of all cake styles, I feel palette-knife designs have become my signature. It's where I feel most inspired. I work with multiple colors to create depth and detail.

Palette knives are stainless steel with wood handles and resemble a small angular metal spatula. They're typically used for acrylic painting. I purchased my knives in a set of 10, which gave me a variety of options for different purposes. For example, a sharp pointed knife works well for leaves. A rounded tip knife works well for petals. A straight edge works well for creating the base of a landscape. A thin narrow knife works well for flower stems.

To create a palette-knife design, it's best to mix all the buttercream colors beforehand. Spread the collection of tinted buttercream on a large metal baking sheet. A flat surface, rather than bowls, is ideal for loading the buttercream onto your palette knife. Place some damp paper towels nearby to wipe your knives in between adding buttercream. Before beginning, chill the cake for 20 minutes to firm up the buttercream base. Using a sweeping motion, load buttercream onto the palette knife. Transfer the buttercream from the knife to the cake by pressing firmly and then lifting away. For a blended look it's not necessary to chill the cake while working. For more crisp lines and color definition, chill the cake every so often to prevent new color additions from blending. Work with dark colors first, then add the highlights.

The Sculpted Buttercream Flower Cake

This technique is similar to a palette-knife cake but heavier and with the focus specifically on flowers. Rather than piping crisp clean

THE PALETTE KNIFE CAKE

flowers with piping tips and bags, I create freestyle sculpted flowers by loading buttercream onto my palette knife and applying it directly onto the cake surface. The flowers are full and highly textured, giving the cake a romantic, vintage feel. For this look, I use a slightly rounded tip or a pointed-tip palette knife.

Like a palette-knife cake, begin by mixing all the buttercream colors beforehand and loading them onto a large metal baking sheet. You'll need a lot of buttercream. Unlike a palette knife cake, where the details are small, a sculpted buttercream flower uses a lot of buttercream to build a three-dimensional petal. To build the petals, scrape the buttercream onto the palette knife, loading most of the buttercream on one side. Transfer the petal to the cake, pressing down firmly then releasing with a subtle dragging motion. Repeat with more petals, alternating the side of the knife that carries the petal weight so the flower looks natural. Halfway through building the flower, add the flower center. Use the same technique but on a smaller scale. Then continue building the flower petals until the flower looks full. Leaves are created with the same method.

The Piped Buttercream Flower Cake

From elegant roses to a garden of bright wildflowers, this style will always be sought after. Buttercream flower cakes can be very realistic if done properly. The key to a beautiful buttercream flower is using the right petal tips. The narrower the tip opening the better, as flower petals themselves are paper thin. I listed my favorite petal tips under Tools of the Trade: Piping Tips (see page 23). I particularly love this style because there are many ways to approach it, from a few statement flowers to a grand floral cascade.

Given the many flower types, I could write a whole book on this subject alone, so I'll only cover the basics here. Mix the colors beforehand. Mixing multiple shades of a color—for example, yellow—and layering those shades within the same piping bag will result in a more realistic-looking flower. Flowers are rarely one solid color. Load piping bags with petal tips and fill them with buttercream. Line baking sheets with parchment paper to store your buttercream flowers. Cut strips of parchment paper 2-inches wide. Then cut those strips into 2-inch squares.

‹

THE SCULPTED BUTTERCREAM FLOWER CAKE

To create a buttercream flower, dab a tiny bit of buttercream onto a metal flower nail. Place a small parchment paper square on top, pressing lightly to secure it. While holding the flower nail by its stem, pipe the flower directly onto the parchment paper square, turning the flower nail with each petal. This will result in a clean, beautiful flower. Piping directly onto the cake does not provide much leverage and will end up being a giant mess. Leaves, however, are easily piped directly onto the cake and work to fill spaces between flowers. While piping, regardless of the flower, think about how nature builds a petal and try to replicate it. Keep the movements swift and sharp. After making a few petals, stop and wipe the piping tip on a damp cloth so there is no buildup of buttercream. This will keep the petals clean. When the flower is finished, transfer the flower on its parchment paper square to the baking sheet. Continue making flowers, varying in size for realism, and when finished, chill them for 30 minutes until firm.

To place the flowers on the cake, use buttercream like glue. Tint

∧
**PIPED
BUTTERCREAM
FLOWERS**

﹥
**THE PIPED
BUTTERCREAM
FLOWER CAKE**

the buttercream "glue" to match either the cake exterior color or the buttercream flower color so it blends in. Load the buttercream "glue" into a piping bag fit with a small round tip, such as a Wilton size 6. Working quickly so your hands don't warm up the chilled buttercream flowers, remove them from the parchment paper and dot the bottoms with buttercream glue. Very carefully, apply the flowers onto the cake in the desired style, pressing gently to secure. Pipe leaves directly onto the cake to fill holes between the flowers. When the design is complete, chill the cake for 20 minutes to firm.

The Textured Cake

A beautifully textured cake can stand alone or serve as a decadent backdrop to a floral design. I find inspiration in Venetian plaster, distressed leather, birch bark, lush velvets, and urban concrete. To create these finishes, I turn to natural earthy colors, such as soft ivory, warm chocolate brown, gun-metal gray, and dusty rose. All these colors to tint buttercream can be found within the wide array of food-gel options. The trick to creating texture lies in how the buttercream is applied. I use metal scrapers, angled spatulas, and occasional palette knives to manipulate buttercream, making it so much more than frosting on a cake.

There are many ways to add texture to a cake. It can be as simple as applying buttercream in a sweeping motion, here and there with an angled spatula, or more complicated with layering buttercream over itself in varying colors to give an impression of depth. Layering is my preferred method as it gives a cake an antiqued look. This technique cannot be accomplished without the use of hot and cold temperatures.

Begin with a fully frosted cake that has been chilled for 20 minutes. Mix the buttercream into varying shades of the same or complementary color. Load an angled spatula with buttercream and apply it to the sides of the cakes in patches, going from top, middle, to bottom, leaving open spaces in between. Heat up a metal scraper under hot water for 5 to 10 seconds and wipe it dry. Use the warm metal scraper to smooth the sides of the cake, wiping off excess buttercream. Chill the cake for 10 minutes to firm up the layer just applied. Then, load your angled spatula with another shade

‹
THE TEXTURED CAKE

of buttercream. Apply the buttercream to the sides of the cake, filling in the open spaces. Some overlap is okay. Use the warm cake scraper to smooth the sides of the cake, wiping off the excess. Repeat these steps until the desired look is achieved.

The Pressed Flower Cake

The most approachable of all styles, but certainly not the least beautiful, is the pressed flower cake. This style can be lush and full or sweet and simple. What I focus on first and foremost is the color palette and mood I want to share. It can be monochromatic, full of rustic woodsy greens, or bright and whimsical. Whatever the vibe, I like to mix in dehydrated flowers or greens with the pressed flowers to add some dimension and life. Just a pop here and there does the trick.

Wonderful sources for pressed and dehydrated flowers can be found on Etsy. These come beautifully preserved and the color varieties are plentiful. Stay within the food-safe variety. But I will warn you, they can be expensive and the shipping times can be long. You can also make your own. This can be done with a traditional flower press or faster with a microwavable flower press, such as the Microfleur. I collect wildflowers during the summer season and shop for flowers at local farmer's markets. I press them myself and keep them in a plastic sheet cover for when they're needed. You can never have too many pressed flowers on hand.

To apply pressed flowers, use an edible adhesive, like Wilton Dab-N-Hold. Using a soft bristle paint brush, brush the back of flowers or greens with the adhesive and place them directly on the cake.

DECORATING WITH BUTTERCREAM

I use American buttercream. American buttercream is a simple blend of unsalted butter, confectioners' sugar, heavy cream, and flavoring. It's my favorite choice for several reasons. It's simple to come together and can be easily flavored. It dries and sets firmly, creating an ideal foundation for decorating. The consistency can be manipulated to create different textures. It colors beautifully. It holds up in warmer weather, which is helpful for summer outdoor weddings. And it tastes delicious. There are other types

›
THE PRESSED
FLOWER CAKE

of buttercream, such as the popular Swiss Meringue or Italian Buttercream. Cake artists prefer one over the other for different reasons. Personally, I like to keep things simple. But I encourage you to experiment with other types to discover what's best for you and suits your creative style.

I use buttercream the same way a painter uses paint on a canvas. I blend colors, mix different consistencies, and add texture and dimension to create unique finishes. A wonderful way to practice with buttercream is to lay out large sheets of parchment paper on your counter. Use the surface to play with different piping tips, mix colors, and test out palette-knife techniques. When you're done you can use a cake scraper to scoop up the buttercream to reuse for more practice.

Bright White Buttercream

Depending on the butter used, the color of American buttercream can vary. Some butters can be more yellow than others; this is determined by where the cows graze and what they eat. A yellow tinted butter isn't bad, just less ideal for getting that crisp white color. I prefer to use Challenge Butter or Land O Lakes Butter because they're pale in color, resulting in a whiter buttercream. However, any butter will do and the final color can be controlled with a few simple adjustments.

The butter should be room temperature but still firm to the touch. In the bowl of a stand mixer on medium-high speed, beat the butter for 3 to 5 minutes. Beating the butter will not only make it light and fluffy, but it lightens the color dramatically, creating the perfect base for crisp white buttercream. Don't forget to scrape down the bowl a couple times while beating.

Add a tiny—and I mean teeny tiny—amount of purple food-gel coloring. Purple is the opposite of yellow on the color wheel. Adding a tiny drop of purple, lavender, or violet will counteract yellow shades coming from the butter. Drop the color onto a rubber spatula rather than directly into the buttercream. This way you can control the amount. You don't want to overdo it and turn your buttercream purple. You can also use the toothpick method described under Tinted Buttercream (see page 42).

^
**TINTED
BUTTERCREAM**

Typically, I don't stray from pure vanilla extract, but if you're looking for a white-as-snow buttercream, pure vanilla extract can darken the color. I use vanilla powder by Nielsen-Massey or Morton & Bassett to flavor my white buttercream. The flavor is natural and delicious. You can also use clear vanilla extract, but be aware it may have an artificial taste.

And finally, to get the brightest white color, add a few drops of white food-gel coloring. But add the white slowly so you don't change the consistency of the buttercream.

After mixing and flavoring, beat the buttercream for another 3 minutes on medium-high speed. Then give it a stir by hand for another 3 minutes to get all those air bubbles out. Use it immediately for best results. The longer it sits the more yellow it will get. Rewhip for a few minutes if needed to bring that bright white back.

Tinted Buttercream

To tint buttercream, I use food gels, both water-based and

oil-based, whichever offers the color shade I'm after. Different manufacturers offer different shades.

For a light color, such as a pale yellow or a rosy pink, I use the toothpick method to tint. This avoids over-saturation. You can always add more color but you can't take color away. Dip the tip of a toothpick into the food-gel container and transfer the color to your buttercream. Add more color if needed.

For a more saturated color, like a deep red or green, I add a drop of color directly from the bottle into the buttercream. Add one drop at a time and mix before adding another, until you've reached the desired color. It's important to note, color develops over time. If you're feeling like you haven't reached the saturation level you want, don't be tempted to drown your buttercream in food gel. It will change the consistency and may become darker than intended. Instead, cover the buttercream with plastic wrap and let it set for 30 to 60 minutes. It will darken as it rests.

Toning Color

Sometimes a color is too bold and bright and needs to be toned down. You can mute a bright color by adding a tiny amount of the contrasting color. This is the color opposite on the color wheel. For example, to mute a bright orange, use the toothpick method to add a little blue. Start small and mix. Add more if needed. Red will mute green, yellow will mute purple, and vice versa.

You can create a wide collection of shades with a basic set of primary color food gels. Add a bit of green to blue to make a teal, or add a touch of yellow to green to make lime. I encourage experimenting; it's the best way to learn. Plus, it's fun.

For piping buttercream details, borders, and flowers, and for palette-knife art, this American buttercream recipe gives you the perfect consistency base. This is not a recipe you'd use to frost a cake; notice there is no heavy cream or salt added. It's purely for decorating and piping. It's a stiff consistency buttercream created to hold its shape and leave wiggle room for adding food-gel coloring.

American Buttercream for Decorating and Piping

MARKS 2 CUPS

- 1 cup unsalted butter, room temperature
- 3 cups confectioners' sugar, sifted
- 1 teaspoon pure vanilla extract

In the bowl of a stand mixer on medium-high speed, beat the butter for 3 to 5 minutes until light and fluffy. Add the confectioners' sugar, 1 cup at a time, mixing well after each addition. Mix in the vanilla. Beat on medium-high speed for 3 more minutes. Continue stirring by hand for another 3 minutes to remove any air bubbles.

Divide the buttercream into separate bowls to add color.

THE PERFECT PIE CRUST PASTRY DOUGH

My mom taught me how to make pie from scratch. She took the craft very seriously, especially during the holiday season. Her apple pie can't be beat. I can still hear her telling me, "Don't let your hands warm up the dough." At the time, I listened without understanding the reasoning behind her teachings. Now, as a professional baker, I understand the science of the practice. Here are my tips for the perfect flaky crust that is both beautiful and delicious:

> There's no arguing that an all-butter crust tastes incredible, but butter doesn't hold up well in the oven. Shortening may be bland, but it doesn't break down as quickly. A crust made with a 1:1 butter-to-shortening ratio is an ideal blend. It will hold its structure without sacrificing flavor.

> Keep your ingredients COLD. Cold ingredients help to maintain the pockets of fats when you roll out the dough. I like to see small pieces of butter still intact. Those butter pockets, when baked, create the flaky layers. Put the butter and shortening in the freezer 30 minutes before adding them to the flour.

> When blending the dough, use your hands as little as possible and don't over mix. The heat from your hands will warm up the fats in the dough and the flaky texture will be lost. I use a pastry blender to combine my dough. You can also use a food processor; however, be careful to not over process. Overworking will cause your dough to be tough. The texture should be crumbly before you add the ice water.

> Add a tablespoon of distilled white vinegar to the ice water. You won't taste it. The vinegar helps tenderize the dough and make it more flaky. Let the ice water sit for 5 minutes before adding it to the dough so it has time to get ice cold.

> Use fine sea salt. Table salt is extremely salty and filled with additives. Sea salt has a clean crisp flavor that won't overpower the flavor of the dough. The fine texture helps it distribute nicely. Kosher salt also works well.

> Roll out the dough on a well-floured surface. Every couple of rolls, rotate the dough 90 degrees so it stays even throughout. Hold the pie dish over the rolled dough and check that you'll have enough to cover the interior with a bit of overhang left over.

> Use the rolling pin to transfer the dough to the pie dish. Place the rolling pin in the center of the rolled dough circle and gently fold the dough over the pin. Lift and place the dough in the pie dish. Press the dough lightly into the interior. Trim the overhanging dough with kitchen shears or a sharp paring knife, or fold over the overhang and crimp the edges in a decorative pattern.

> Once the pie crust is filled, styled, and oven ready, add a heavy cream wash to the dough edges and the top using a pastry brush. Traditionally bakers will add an egg wash to a pie before baking, but I prefer brushing the edges and top with heavy cream. The fat from the cream creates a luxurious golden brown and also adds shiny sheen. After brushing the edges with heavy cream, add a generous sprinkle of coarse sugar to the dough to add sparkle and a sweet finish.

> If you notice the crust browning too much while baking, remove it from the oven and cover the edges of the pie dish with aluminum foil and then return to the oven.

HIGH-ALTITUDE BAKING

If you're a baker in a mountain town, you've no doubt experienced the frustrating effects of high altitude. Looks perfect coming out of the oven, but within minutes the center falls, the edges crack, it becomes dry and hard as rock. I learned this lesson the hard way during a family trip to Mammoth, California, where the 7,880-foot elevation murdered my fail-proof red velvet cupcakes. Everyone still ate them, because, let's be honest, a bad cupcake is better than no cupcake. I drowned them in cream cheese frosting and received no complaints. But the experience left me disappointed and confused. I had made this recipe a dozen times; what happened? It was then I realized the majority of recipes are created for sea-level living.

When I moved to Jackson Hole, which is roughly 6,500 feet above sea level, I was hesitant to bake anything for months. I didn't want to spend the time and effort only to have something not turn out. I even made my son's birthday cake from a box, which is a road I've never traveled down before. But as I settled in, and the nights grew cold and cozy, I wanted to bake. For me, baking is joy. So I determined to make high attitude my friend.

I talked to neighbors, I researched, I watched cooking shows, I got scientific. And I baked. I tested techniques, methods, and ingredients; cookies, cupcakes, scones, cakes—the works. My husband and boys had never been happier. Finally, I figured it out. You can bake everything you've always loved at high elevation. It's simply a matter of understanding the basic fundamentals of how ingredients come together . . . and a little science.

It all comes down to water and atmospheric pressure. At high altitude, the atmospheric pressure is less than at sea level, so water responds differently. For every 1,000 feet you climb, the boiling point of water drops roughly 2 degrees F/1 degree C. For example, at sea level water boils at 212 degrees F/100 degrees C, at 3,000 feet above sea level, water boils at 206 degrees F/97 degrees C. In Jackson Hole we're at 6,500 feet, so the boiling point is 200 degrees F/94 degrees C.

When baking a cake, for example, an internal temperature (190 to 250 degrees F) needs to be reached in order for the cake to set. This is where the trouble with

sea-level recipes begins. A climb in elevation causes the boiling point of water to decrease. So water is evaporating at a faster rate and lower temperature. Hence the cracking and drying. Less atmospheric pressure is causing the cake to rise faster. The chemical leaveners—baking powder and baking soda—are accelerated. The cake rises before hitting the needed internal temperature to set. Hence the dreaded collapse.

The recipes in this book are written for a general audience, but for those baking at altitude, adjust the ingredients to compensate for water evaporation and low atmospheric pressure:

LIQUID You're losing liquid faster so simply add more. At 3,000 feet, add 1 to 2 tablespoons of water. For every additional 1,000 feet, add 1 tablespoon more.

SUGAR Sugar binds to water. The loss of water makes the sugar, in basic terms, more intense. At 3,000 feet and higher, decrease the sugar by 1 tablespoon per cup of sugar.

CHEMICAL LEAVENER High altitude pushes baking powder and baking soda into high speed. At 3,000 feet, decrease the leaveners by ⅛ teaspoon. At 5,000 feet, by ¼ teaspoon. At 6,000 feet or above, decrease by ½ teaspoon.

OVEN TEMPERATURE Increase the oven temperature to help baked goods set as they rise. At 3,000 feet increase by 15 degrees F. At 6,000 feet and above increase by 25 degrees F.

BAKING TIME Because you're raising the temperature, start checking for doneness about 5 minutes sooner.

FLOUR Adding flour will give the cake more structure. At 3,000 feet increase the flour by 1 tablespoon. Add 1 tablespoon for every additional 1,500 feet.

EGGS Protein creates setting power. Add an egg.

Keep in mind these adjustments are starting points. Baking isn't an exact science. All ovens are different; all ingredients are different. You'll have to test each recipe and find what works. But these changes will get you to where you want to be. Be patient and have fun!

The Four Seasons

MY HOMETOWN OF SAN CLEMENTE, California, is known for having the best climate in the world. Days are 75 degrees F, rain is rare, and the sun is always shining. For most people, this would be a dream. But I spent the first thirty-five years of my life in that setting and I longed for change. I'd see movies with kids raking leaves and cozy winter-wonderland towns that looked like the insides of snow globes. The changing of seasons . . . I always wondered what that would be like.

Living in Wyoming, now I know. And it's everything I hoped it would be. When a change of season sets in, it's like closing one book and opening a new one. The weather changes, the smells change, the colors change, the activities change. *You* change. It awakens a different part of your soul. For me, the seasons inspire my art and my cooking. I associate each season in its own way with certain flavors, styles, and baking traditions.

Spring

SPRING IS FILLED WITH EXCITEMENT AND ENERGY. You hibernate all winter long, bundled up with heavy coats, thick socks, and snow boots. All you've seen is white for miles. Spring is when you wake up. You start to see color again: blades of grass peeking through and wildflowers budding everywhere. There's this explosion of life after you've been shut in for months. Growth is happening, the animals start coming out, the sun warms your skin. It's like nature is throwing a party and everyone is invited.

As the snow slowly melts away, color rolls in like a happy, playful dance. You see soft purples and pinks in the wildflowers, bright green in the aspens, pale grays in the river rocks, and muted browns and sage from the mountain base. Spring awakens my artistic palette and these colors show up in my work. I'm inspired by rustic textures, florals, and citrus. I crave apricots, raspberries, pistachios, spiced snickerdoodles, and my favorite carrot cake cupcakes. Spring is when I start collecting wildflowers to press for decorating cakes and cookies. It's when my creativity is most alive, ready for a fresh beginning.

DECORATING WITH NATURE

MOTHER NATURE IS the original artist. Her creations are sprinkled throughout the planet, waiting to be swept up and replicated. She is the master of color, proportion, balance, and invention and the foundation from which all artistic endeavors evolve. You can see her effortless style in a field of perfectly imperfect wild flowers. Her seduction and glamour in the unveiling of a ripe red rose. Her intensity and grit in the jagged-edged bark of a winter aspen tree. And her mystery and depth in the wild rapids of a rushing river. She has so much to teach and share. When I create, it's my humble way of letting her know I'm listening.

FLOWERS

Each one an individual masterpiece, flowers are my favorite natural decor. Offering a never-ending palette of color, flowers set a mood. There are multiple ways to utilize flowers: fresh, pressed, and dried. A cascade of fresh English roses or peonies speak to timeless elegance, genuine and classic. Layered pressed violas and daisies create Bohemian romance, turning a cake into a vintage canvas, like a still-life Van Gogh painting. A mix of aged dried flowers make a bespoke statement, with dimension, antiquity, and texture. Bringing life to a cake, flowers will always be in fashion.

I've found it's best to approach their use freely, with a no-rules mentality.

HERBS AND SPICES

For a rustic, woodland feel, I love to add herbs and spices to my cakes and baked goods, especially during the holiday season. A sprig of fresh rosemary or thyme mimics the look of forest trees, cinnamon sticks become a bundle of firewood, and star anise reflects a snowflake or a starry night. These rough, earthy elements bring warmth and nostalgia to desserts, creating a gorgeous contrast to smooth silky buttercream.

BERRIES, CITRUS, AND DRIED FRUITS

When decorating with berries, citrus, and dried fruits, you're teasing with a visual description of what awaits inside, like an invitation. I take the natural beauty and unique outline of fruits and use them in unexpected ways. I like to enhance the texture of berries by rolling them in coarse sugar or edible gold luster dust. It creates the look of precious jewels. With sliced blood oranges and limes, I play with radiating geometry and pattern. I arrange dehydrated pineapple and apples like floral arrangements. The possibilities are limitless, and best of all, delicious.

GOLD, SILVER, AND COPPER

Like a piece of jewelry that finishes a look, I use natural metallics to add luster, decadence, and shine. Edible and worth every penny, metallics are available in thin sheets, dust, and sprinkles. Gold leaf pops beautifully against dark chocolate, silver luster dust adds a wintery highlight to crisp white buttercream edges, and flecks of copper bring warmth to florals and painted ombré finishes.

NUTS

Tiny pieces come together to create a bigger picture. Finely ground, chopped, or whole, nuts are an enticing enhancement to any dessert. I especially love pistachios with their vibrant earthy green. I sprinkle them in the center of buttercream flowers to make them more lifelike. Pecans and walnuts, with their natural intricate design, make a statement all their own when arranged on pies and cake tops. When I want something heavy and robust, I turn to whole roasted hazelnuts.

LANDSCAPES, WILDLIFE, AND TREES

Oscar Wilde said, "Imitation is the sincerest form of flattery." I hope Mother Nature feels this way as I flatter her with everything I create, mainly with the use of landscapes, wildlife, and trees. I paint her settings on my cakes and cookies, in buttercream and food coloring, inspired by the season we're in, in the hope that I can transport people somewhere beautiful. From mountainscapes to desert scenes, sunrise to sunset, there's no end to the options. Bison, elk, and deer are my favorite animals to paint. I've witnessed them migrating and feel a connection to them deep in my soul.

Hummingbird Cake with Spiced Rum Buttercream

This charming spiced banana cake is a breeze to make and serves a crowd, making it perfect for spring celebrations. The recipe can be easily halved for a smaller cake or cupcakes. I love the addition of spiced rum, which adds just the right amount of warmth and highlights the banana flavors. This cake looks beautiful, decorated naturally with dried pineapple and wildflowers.

MAKES 1 (3-LAYER 9-INCH) CAKE

FOR THE HUMMINGBIRD CAKE

4½ cups all-purpose flour

3 cups granulated sugar

1½ teaspoons baking soda

1½ teaspoons salt

2 teaspoons ground cinnamon

½ teaspoon ground allspice

1½ cups vegetable oil

4 large eggs, room temperature

2 teaspoons pure vanilla extract

3 cups mashed overripe bananas (from 4 to 5 bananas)

1 (12-ounce) can crushed pineapple, well drained

1½ cups chopped toasted pecans

⅓ cup spiced rum

FOR THE SPICED RUM BUTTERCREAM

1½ cups unsalted butter, room temperature

1 (8-ounce) block full-fat cream cheese, room temperature

5½ cups confectioners' sugar, sifted

1 teaspoon pure vanilla extract

2 to 3 tablespoons spiced rum

¼ teaspoon kosher salt

FOR ASSEMBLY

Toasted pecans

Wildflowers for decorating

Dried Pineapple Flowers (see sidebar on page 58)

Preheat the oven to 350 degrees F. Butter 3 (9-inch) round cake pans. Line the bottom of the pans with parchment paper. Dust the interior of the pans generously with flour, then tip over to knock out the excess, leaving a thin coating.

To make the cake, in a large bowl, whisk the flour, sugar, baking soda, salt, cinnamon, and allspice to blend. In another bowl, whisk together the oil, eggs, and vanilla. Add the egg mixture to the dry ingredients and whisk to combine, making sure no lumps of dry ingredients remain. Using a wooden spoon or rubber spatula, stir in the bananas, pineapple, and pecans until combined. Add the spiced rum and stir to combine. The batter will be thick and heavy. Divide the batter equally between the prepared

continued >

pans. Bake for 30 to 35 minutes or until a tester inserted into the center of the cakes comes out clean. Cool the cakes in the pans for 10 minutes. Run a knife around the cake sides and turn out onto a wire rack to cool completely.

To make the buttercream, in the bowl of an electric mixer on medium-high speed, beat the butter and cream cheese until light and fluffy, about 3 minutes. With the mixer on low speed, add the confectioners' sugar, 1 cup at a time. Scrape down the bowl as needed. Add the vanilla, spiced rum, and salt. Mix on medium speed until well combined, about 3 minutes.

To assemble the cake, place one cooled cake layer on a cake plate, flat side facing down. Add a heaping ½ cup of buttercream to the top. Using an offset spatula, spread the buttercream evenly to the edges. Top with a second cake layer. Repeat with another layer of buttercream, spreading evenly to the edges.

Top with the final cake layer, flat side facing up. Add a heaping ½ cup of buttercream to the top. Using an offset spatula, spread buttercream evenly to the edges.

Using the offset spatula, add any remaining frosting to the sides of the cake to fill in gaps between layers. Then smooth to create a semi-naked finish. Place the cake

in the refrigerator to chill for 15 minutes before decorating. Decorate with toasted pecans, wildflowers, and dried pineapple flowers.

DRIED PINEAPPLE FLOWERS

1 ripe pineapple

Preheat the oven to 225 degrees F. Line a baking sheet with parchment paper. Trim the outer skin of the pineapple. Using a sharp knife, slice the pineapple into ¼-inch disks, no thicker. Lay the disks flat and add 5 more cuts, divided evenly around the perimeter, going from the outside and stopping at the center core of the pineapple slice, to create flower petals. Spread the disks on the prepared baking sheet in an even layer, 2 inches apart. Bake 2 to 3 hours, flipping halfway through, until they're dried and very lightly browned around the edges. While the pineapples are still warm, place each one in the cup of a cupcake tin. Press down at their center, into the cup, so the petals curl up, creating the flower. Let them dry completely in the cupcake tin for at least 1 hour.

Almond Cake with Crushed Sugared Blackberries and Rich Chocolate Buttercream

MAKES 1 (3-LAYER 6-INCH) CAKE

FOR THE ALMOND CAKE

- 1½ cups all-purpose flour
- ¾ cup almond flour, preferably superfine
- 2 teaspoons baking powder
- 1 teaspoon kosher salt
- ¾ cup unsalted butter, room temperature
- 1½ cups granulated sugar
- 3 large eggs, room temperature
- 1½ teaspoons pure vanilla extract
- ¾ teaspoon pure almond extract
- 1 cup whole milk, room temperature

Fresh blackberries, for decorating

FOR THE SUGARED BLACKBERRIES

- 2 cups fresh blackberries
- 1 tablespoon granulated sugar
- 1 tablespoon Grand Marnier

FOR THE RICH-CHOCOLATE BUTTERCREAM

- 1½ cups unsalted butter, at room temperature
- ¾ cup high-quality Dutch-process cocoa powder such as Ghirardelli or Guittard, sifted
- 5 cups confectioners' sugar, sifted
- 3 teaspoons pure vanilla extract
- ⅓ cup heavy cream, plus more if needed
- ¼ teaspoon kosher salt

Preheat the oven to 350 degrees F. Butter 3 (6-inch) cake pans. Line the bottoms with parchment paper. Dust the interior of the pans generously with flour, then tip over to knock out the excess, leaving a thin coating.

To make the cake, in a medium bowl, sift together the all-purpose flour, almond flour, baking powder, and salt. Set aside. In the bowl of an electric mixer on medium speed, cream the butter and sugar together until light and fluffy, about 3 minutes. On low speed, add the eggs, one at a time, mixing well after each addition. Scrape down the bowl. Add the vanilla and almond extracts. Mix well, about 1 minute.

On low speed, slowly add half of the dry ingredients, followed by half of the milk. Scrape down the bowl. Repeat with the remaining dry ingredients and milk. Mix until just combined. Divide the batter evenly between the cake pans. Bake for 30 to 35 minutes, or until a tester inserted into the center of the cakes comes out clean. Cool the cakes in the pans for 10 minutes. Run a knife around the cake sides and turn out onto a wire rack to cool completely.

continued >

To make the sugared blackberries, in a medium bowl, combine the blackberries, sugar, and Grand Marnier. Using a wooden spoon, toss the ingredients together to coat, then lightly crush the blackberries. Set aside. Be sure to give a final toss before using.

To make the buttercream, in the bowl of an electric mixer fitted with a paddle attachment on medium-high speed, beat the butter on until light and fluffy, 3 to 5 minutes. Add the sifted cocoa. Mix until combined. Add the confectioners' sugar, one cup at a time, mixing well after each addition. Add the vanilla extract, ⅓ cup cream, and salt. Mix until combined. If the buttercream is too thick, add 1 to 2 tablespoons more cream. Scrape down the bowl. Then mix on medium speed for 3 minutes until the frosting is light and fluffy.

To assemble the cake, place one cooled cake layer on a cake plate, flat side facing down. Cover the top with a generous layer of chocolate buttercream. Add a spoonful of crushed blackberries, leaving a 1-inch border around the cake edges. You don't want the blackberries leaking out of the sides.

Place the second cake layer, flat side facing up, on top of the frosted first layer. Fill the gaps between the cake layers with buttercream. Repeat the steps with the buttercream and blackberries. Place the final cake layer, flat side facing up. Cover the top and sides of the cake with a thin coat of buttercream to lock in the crumbs. Place the uncovered cake in the refrigerator to chill for 15 minutes. Remove the cake from the fridge and, with an offset spatula, apply a generous layer of buttercream frosting over the entire cake, starting at the top and smoothing down and over the sides. Top with fresh blackberries.

NOTE: I used edible gold luster dust to paint the highlights on the chocolate buttercream. You mix a dime-size amount of dust with a drop or two of vodka to make a thick paste. The vodka evaporates, leaving the gold behind. Make sure the buttercream is firm and chilled before adding painted details. For a dramatic blackberry drip, lightly push some of the crushed blackberries and their juices over the cake edge so the juices drip down the side. I also brushed the gold paint on the exterior of the blackberries. Luster dusts can be found at local craft stores or online.

Lemon-Rhubarb Poppy Seed Squares

MAKES 12 BARS

FOR THE LEMON POPPY SEED CRUST

- 2 cups plus 3 tablespoons all-purpose flour
- ½ cup granulated sugar
- ½ teaspoon kosher salt
- 1 cup unsalted butter, well chilled and cut into small cubes
- 1 teaspoon pure vanilla extract
- 1 tablespoon freshly grated lemon zest
- 1 tablespoon poppy seeds

LEMON-RHUBARB FILLING

- 3 cups sliced rhubarb
- 1¼ cups granulated sugar, divided
- 3 tablespoons fresh lemon juice, plus ¾ cup more, divided
- ¼ teaspoon kosher salt
- 3 tablespoons all-purpose flour
- 3 large eggs, room temperature

Preheat the oven to 350 degrees F. Butter an 8 x 10-inch pan and line with parchment paper. Allow the parchment paper to hang over the edge of the pan so that you can pull the bars out easily after baking.

To make the crust, in a food processor, combine the flour, sugar, and salt. Pulse until combined. Add the cubed butter and vanilla extract. Pulse until the mixture resembles coarse crumbs. Add the lemon zest and poppy seeds. Pulse until just combined. Using your fingers or a rubber spatula, firmly press the dough into the prepared pan, spreading evenly

to coat the bottom. Bake for 20 minutes, until lightly browned. Set aside to cool as you make the filling.

To make the filling, in a medium saucepan over medium heat, combine the rhubarb, ¾ cup sugar, and 3 tablespoons lemon juice. Bring the mixture to a boil, stirring occasionally. Simmer until the sugar is fully dissolved and the rhubarb has softened, about 5 minutes. Set aside to cool for 10 minutes.

Pour the cooled rhubarb mixture into a food processor. Process until very smooth. Add the salt, remaining ½ cup sugar, and ¾ cup lemon juice. Process until smooth, stopping to scrape the sides if needed. Add the flour. Pulse until combined. With the processor running, add the eggs, one at a time. Process until smooth. The mixture should be a pale pink. Pour the mixture over the crust. Bake for 20 to 23 minutes, or until the center is set. Cool on a wire rack for 1 hour, then cover and refrigerate for at least 2 hours until firm. Using the parchment paper sides, lift out of the pan. Cut into twelve bars.

NOTES: These bars are best enjoyed the day they're made, but will last for 2 to 3 days kept covered and chilled. To ensure a rich rhubarb color, use the darkest part of the rhubarb stem.

Vanilla Shortbread Cookies with Pressed Flowers

Pansies and daisies are my favorite edible flowers for cookies. They're beautiful, hold up through baking, and have a mild flavor. I have these flowers growing in my garden and love to press them myself, using a traditional flower press. They can be easily found online. Etsy is a great source. Just make sure they're safe for culinary use.

MAKES 24 TO 30 COOKIES

1 **cup unsalted butter, room temperature**
½ **cup confectioners' sugar, sifted**
1 **teaspoon vanilla bean paste**
½ **cup cornstarch**
2 **cups all-purpose flour, plus more for rolling**
½ **teaspoon kosher salt**
Edible pressed flowers
Coarse sugar

Line two baking sheets with parchment paper.

In the bowl of an electric mixer on medium speed, beat the butter and confectioners' sugar until combined, about 3 minutes. Add the vanilla bean paste. Mix to combine.

In a large bowl, sift the cornstarch, 2 cups flour, and salt together. Add the dry ingredients to the butter-sugar mixture, mixing until just combined. On a well-floured surface, roll the dough out to ¼- to ⅜-inch-thick. Cut into desired shapes. Using a spatula, transfer the cookies to the prepared baking sheets, placing them 2 inches apart. Top each cookie with a pressed flower, pressing lightly to adhere. Lightly sprinkle with coarse sugar. Place the baking sheets in the refrigerator to chill for at least 1 hour. This helps the cookies hold their shape while baking.

Preheat the oven to 350 degrees F. Remove the baking sheets from the refrigerator and then bake for 10 to 12 minutes, until firm and crisp around the edges. Allow the cookies to cool for 5 minutes on the baking sheets before transferring them to a wire rack to cool completely. The cookies will keep in an airtight container for 1 week.

Chocolate Shortbread

MAKES 24 TO 30 COOKIES

1 cup unsalted butter, room temperature

1 cup confectioners' sugar, sifted

1 teaspoon vanilla bean paste

½ cup cocoa powder, sifted

2 cups all-purpose flour, plus more for rolling

½ teaspoon kosher salt

Pressed violas (pansies) or daisies for decorating

Coarse sugar for sprinkling

Line two baking sheets with parchment paper.

In the bowl of an electric mixer on medium speed, beat the butter and confectioners' sugar until combined, about 3 minutes. Add the vanilla bean paste. Mix to combine.

In a large bowl, sift the cocoa, 2 cups flour, and salt together. Add the dry ingredients to the butter-sugar mixture, mixing until just combined. On a well-floured surface, roll the dough out to ¼- to ⅜-inch-thick. Cut into desired shapes. Using a spatula, transfer the cookies to the prepared baking sheets, placing them 2 inches apart. Top each cookie with pressed flowers, pressing lightly to adhere. Lightly sprinkle with coarse sugar. Place the baking sheets in the refrigerator to chill for at least 1 hour. This helps the cookies hold their shape while baking.

Preheat the oven to 350 degrees F. Remove the baking sheets from the refrigerator and then bake for 10 to 12 minutes, until firm and crisp around the edges. Allow the cookies to cool for 5 minutes on the baking sheets before transferring them to a wire rack to cool completely. The cookies will keep in an airtight container for 1 week.

Apricot and Raspberry Pie

MAKES 1 (9-INCH) DOUBLE-CRUST PIE

FOR THE CRUST

2½ cups all-purpose flour

1 tablespoon granulated sugar

1 teaspoon kosher salt

1 cup unsalted butter, well chilled and cut into cubes

1 tablespoon apple cider vinegar

½ cup ice water, plus a few tablespoons more if needed

FOR THE FILLING

¼ cup cornstarch

¾ cup granulated sugar

¼ teaspoon kosher salt

Pinch of freshly grated nutmeg

1½ pounds (8 large) ripe apricots, cut into ½-inch wedges

2 cups fresh raspberries

1 teaspoon freshly squeezed lemon juice

2 tablespoons Grand Marnier liqueur

Heavy cream for brushing

Coarse sugar for sprinkling

Vanilla ice cream (optional)

Vanilla whipped cream (optional)

To make the crust, in a large bowl, mix the flour, sugar, and salt. Add the cubed butter. With a pastry blender, or your fingertips, blend until the mixture begins to resemble small peas. Mix the apple cider vinegar into the ice water. Drizzle a few tablespoons of water over the flour and butter mixture. Use a fork to mix, adding more water until the dough begins to come together. Once the dough becomes moist and clumps together, it's hydrated

continued >

enough. Divide the dough into 2 balls. Flatten them into disks and wrap them in plastic wrap. Chill for 1 hour and up to 2 days.

Remove the dough from the refrigerator 30 minutes before you're ready to use so it will roll out easily.

Preheat the oven to 425 degrees F.

Roll out 1 disk of dough on a well-floured surface to a 12- to 13-inch circle. The dough should be larger than the pie dish. Carefully transfer the dough to the pie dish. (I fold the dough over my rolling pin to make it easier.) Gently press the dough into the sides of the dish, leaving 1 inch of overhang on the sides. Trim and crimp the edges decoratively. Refrigerate while you prepare the filling.

To make the filling, in a large bowl, whisk together the cornstarch, sugar, salt, and nutmeg. Add the sliced apricots, raspberries, lemon juice, and Grand Marnier. Using a wooden spoon, gently toss together to coat, being careful not to break up the raspberries.

Remove the chilled pie crust from the refrigerator. Pour in the fruit filling, gently spreading evenly to the edges. Return to the fridge. Roll out the remaining pie dough disk. You can either keep the dough whole and place over the top of the filling, or slice into strips for a decorative lattice pie crust. Remove the chilled pie from the refrigerator. Cover the top of the pie with the dough. If keeping it whole, cut 4 to 5 slits in the top to vent. Fold the overhanging dough over the top and crimp the sides together. Using a pastry brush, brush the edges and top with the heavy cream.

Bake for 15 minutes, then reduce the temperature to 375 degrees F. Bake for 35 minutes more. Carefully pull the pie out of the oven and generously sprinkle the edges and top with coarse sugar. Continue baking for another 10 to 15 minutes, until the crust is golden brown and the filling is bubbling. Allow the pie to cool for 2 hours before serving with vanilla ice cream or vanilla whipped cream, if using.

Peanut Butter and Chocolate Cookie Sandwiches

MAKES 18 GIANT COOKIE SANDWICHES, MAKES 1½ CUPS GANACHE

FOR THE COOKIES

- 2¼ cups all-purpose flour
- ½ teaspoon baking soda
- ½ teaspoon baking powder
- 1 teaspoon kosher salt
- 1 cup unsalted butter, room temperature
- 1 cup granulated sugar, divided
- 1 cup firmly packed light brown sugar
- 2 large eggs, room temperature
- 2 teaspoons pure vanilla extract
- 1 heaping cup creamy peanut butter
- 1 cup roasted salted peanuts, chopped

FOR THE PEANUT BUTTER-CHOCOLATE GANACHE

- 1¼ cups finely chopped high-quality milk, semisweet, or dark chocolate
- ⅓ cup creamy salted peanut butter
- ¾ cup heavy cream
- Pinch of kosher salt

To make the cookies, in a medium bowl, whisk together the flour, baking soda, baking powder and salt. In the bowl of an electric mixer on medium-high speed, cream the butter, ½ cup granulated sugar, and brown sugar until light and fluffy, about 3 minutes. With the mixer on low, add the eggs, one at a time, mixing well after each addition and then add the vanilla extract. Add the peanut butter. With the mixer on low, add the dry ingredients, mixing until just combined. Stir in the peanuts. Place the dough in the refrigerator for at least 60 minutes.

Preheat the oven to 350 degrees F. Line two baking sheets with parchment paper.

Place the remaining ½ cup granulated sugar in a small bowl. Roll the chilled dough into 1½-inch balls then lightly roll in the sugar to coat. Place them on the prepared baking sheets, about 2 inches apart. With a fork, press the cookies flat using a crisscross pattern. Bake for 12 to 13 minutes, until the cookies are lightly browned on the edges. Allow the cookies to cool for 5 minutes, then transfer to a wire rack to cool completely.

To make the ganache, place the chopped chocolate and peanut butter in a heatproof bowl. In a medium saucepan, bring the cream to a simmer. Pour the simmering cream over the chocolate and peanut butter. Cover with aluminum foil and let it set for 2 minutes. Then whisk until smooth. Stir in the salt. The ganache will thicken as it sets. Reheat if necessary for a pourable consistency.

To assemble the cookies, add a heaping spoonful of room-temperature peanut butter–chocolate ganache to the flat side of a cookie. Spread gently to the edges, making a level layer. Top with a second cookie, flat side down. Press firmly together. Store the cookies in an airtight container for up to 5 days.

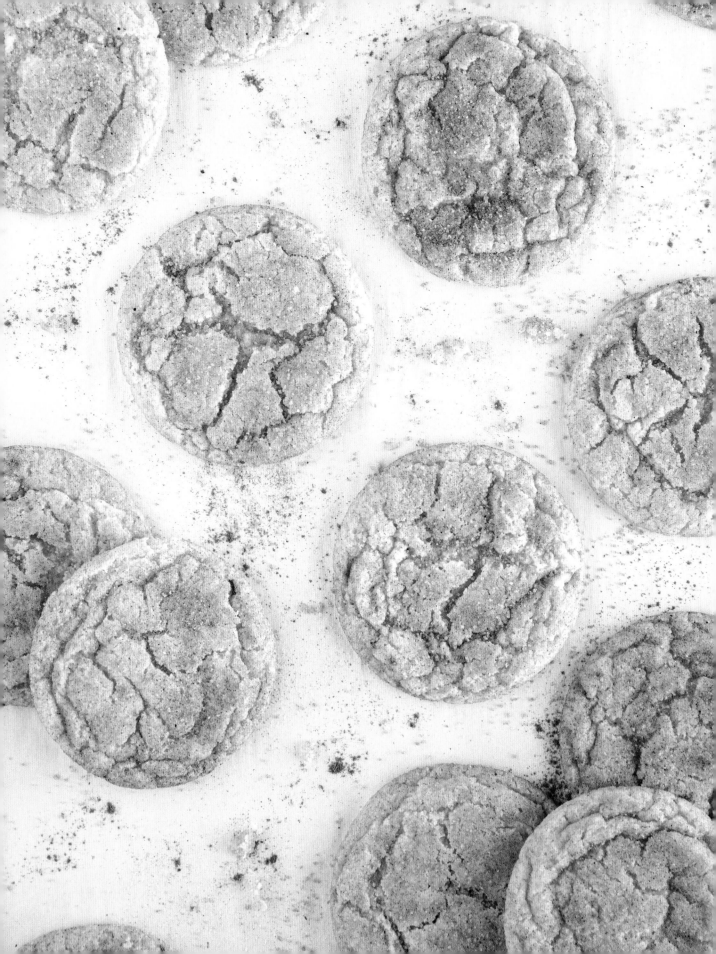

Old-Fashioned Snickerdoodles

MAKES ABOUT 24 TO 30 COOKIES

2½ cups all-purpose flour

2 teaspoons cream of tartar

1 teaspoon baking soda

⅛ teaspoon freshly grated nutmeg

1 teaspoon kosher salt

¾ cup unsalted butter, room temperature

¼ cup vegetable shortening

1¾ cups granulated sugar, divided

1 egg, room temperature

1 egg yolk, room temperature

1 tablespoon vanilla extract

2 teaspoons ground cinnamon

Preheat the oven to 375 degrees F. Line two baking sheets with parchment paper.

Mix the flour, cream of tartar, baking soda, nutmeg, and salt in a medium bowl. Set aside. In the bowl of an electric mixer on medium speed, cream the butter, shortening, and 1½ cups sugar until light and fluffy, about 2 minutes. Scrape down the bowl as needed. Add the egg, egg yolk, and vanilla extract. Mix until combined. With the mixer on low speed, add the dry ingredients. Mix until just combined.

In a small bowl, mix the remaining ¼ cup sugar and the cinnamon together. Working with 2 tablespoons at a time, roll the dough into balls. Roll each ball in the sugar and cinnamon mixture to coat. Place on the baking sheets 2 to 3 inches apart. Bake for 10 minutes, making sure to reverse the positions of the baking sheets in the oven from front to back, upper to lower, halfway through baking. The cookies should look set on the outside and soft and puffy in the middle. Let the cookies cool and set for 5 minutes on the baking sheets before transferring to a wire rack to cool completely.

NOTE: The cookies will flatten and spread in the oven. I keep a dinner spoon handy to gently push the edges in, keeping the cookies nice and round. This must be done immediately after removing the cookies from the oven.

Chewy White Chocolate-Brown Butter Blondies

MAKES 12 BARS

2¾ cups all-purpose flour

1 teaspoon baking soda

1 teaspoon cornstarch

1 teaspoon kosher salt

¾ cup unsalted butter, browned and cooled (see sidebar)

1¾ cups packed light brown sugar

2 large eggs, room temperature

1 large egg yolk, room temperature

2 teaspoons pure vanilla extract

1 cup toffee bits

1 cup toasted chopped walnuts

1½ cups chopped high-quality white chocolate such as Ghirardelli or Guittard

Salted Caramel Sauce, for drizzling (see page 78)

Preheat the oven to 350 degrees F. Line an 8 x 10-inch pan with parchment paper, leaving a 1-inch overhang on each side. This allows you to get the bars out easily for cutting.

In a medium bowl, whisk together the flour, baking soda, cornstarch, and salt. Set aside.

In a large bowl, whisk together the browned butter and brown sugar until combined. Add the eggs, egg yolk, and vanilla. Whisk until smooth. Pour the dry ingredients into the wet ingredients. Stir with a wooden spoon until just combined. Add the toffee bits, walnuts, and white chocolate. Stir until everything comes together. Pour the batter into the prepared pan, pressing it evenly to the edges. Bake for 25 to 27 minutes, until the edges and top have lightly browned. Remove the pan from the oven and place on a wire rack. Allow the bars to cool completely in the pan before lifting out and cutting. Drizzle with salted caramel sauce to serve.

Store blondies in an airtight container for up to 5 days.

HOW TO BROWN BUTTER

Place sticks of unsalted butter in a medium skillet. Melt the butter over medium heat, whisking constantly for 5 to 6 minutes. The butter will foam up and begin to smell nutty. It will change to a light brown color and you'll see light brown colored specks at the bottom of the pan. Pour the butter into a heatproof bowl, making sure to get all the browned specks. If using the butter melted, set aside and let it cool to room temperature. If using as a solid, chill in the refrigerator for at least 4 hours or overnight then let it sit out at room temperature for 1 hour before using.

continued >

Salted Caramel Sauce

MAKES ABOUT 1½ CUPS

1 cup sugar
½ tablespoon water
6 tablespoons unsalted butter, cut into cubes, room temperature
½ cup heavy cream, room temperature
1 teaspoon kosher salt or sea salt

In a large saucepan on medium-high heat, combine the sugar and water and stir constantly until the sugar is melted, about 5 minutes. Once all the sugar has dissolved, add the butter. Continue stirring, being careful not to let the mixture burn. The mixture will boil up. Once the butter has melted, stir to combine completely and then turn the heat to medium low. With a whisk, slowly add the cream. Continue whisking until the mixture turns a golden brown. Remove from the heat. Stir in the salt. Set aside and cool for 5 minutes. The sauce will begin to thicken. Refrigerate for 30 minutes until fully thickened and ready to use. The caramel sauce will keep, refrigerated, in an airtight container for up to 2 weeks.

NOTES: For a bourbon whiskey caramel, stir in 2 to 3 tablespoons of your favorite bourbon whiskey along with the salt. I favor Wyoming Whiskey. For a vanilla bean caramel, add only ½ teaspoon salt and stir in 1 teaspoon vanilla bean paste. For an espresso caramel, add only ½ teaspoon salt and stir in ½ teaspoon ground espresso powder.

Coffee-Break Brownies

MAKES 18 BROWNIES

FOR THE BROWNIE LAYER

- ¾ cup unsalted butter
- 4 ounces bittersweet chocolate, chopped
- 2 teaspoons ground espresso powder
- 2 cups granulated sugar
- 3 large eggs, room temperature
- 2 teaspoons pure vanilla extract
- 1 cup unsweetened Dutch-process cocoa powder
- 1 teaspoon kosher salt
- 1 cup all-purpose flour
- 1 cup semisweet or bittersweet chocolate chips

FOR THE CREAM CHEESE LAYER

- 8 ounces full-fat cream cheese, room temperature
- 6 tablespoons unsalted butter, room temperature
- 1½ cups confectioners' sugar, sifted
- 1½ teaspoons vanilla bean paste
- ½ teaspoon ground cinnamon

FOR THE ESPRESSO GLAZE

- 6 ounces bittersweet chocolate, finely chopped
- 2 tablespoons unsalted butter
- ½ cup heavy cream
- 1 teaspoon ground espresso powder

Pinch of kosher salt

Preheat the oven to 350 degrees F. Line a 9 x 13-inch pan with parchment paper, leaving a 1-inch overhang on each side. This allows you to get the bars out easily for cutting.

continued >

To make the brownie layer, in a large heatproof bowl set over a pan of barely simmering water over medium-low heat, warm the butter and chocolate. Stir until melted and smooth. Stir in the espresso powder. Allow to cool for 10 minutes.

Add the sugar to the butter mix, whisking until well combined. Add the eggs and vanilla, whisking until well combined. Using a wooden spoon, add the cocoa, salt, and flour and mix until well combined. Stir in the chocolate chips. The batter will be thick. Bake for 25 to 27 minutes. Begin testing with a toothpick at 25 minutes. If you see a couple of moist crumbs on the toothpick, the brownies are perfect. Allow the brownies to cool in the pan, on a wire rack, for at least 1 hour, or until they're no longer warm to the touch.

To make the cream cheese layer, in the bowl of an electric mixer on medium speed, beat the cream cheese and butter until light and fluffy, about 2 minutes.

Add the confectioners' sugar, ½ cup at a time, mixing well after each addition. Add the vanilla bean paste and cinnamon. Mix for 1 minute until well combined. With a rubber spatula, spread the cream cheese mixture over the cooled brownies in an even layer. Refrigerate until firm, about 1 hour.

To make the espresso glaze, in a medium heatproof bowl set over a pan of barely simmering water combine the chopped chocolate, butter, cream, espresso powder, and salt. Over medium-low heat, stir until melted and smooth. Remove from the heat and cool until it is room temperature but still pourable, about 15 minutes. Pour the glaze over the brownies. Cover and refrigerate for at least 3 hours, or until the glaze has set. Serve chilled or at room temperature.

These brownies will keep, refrigerated, in an airtight container for up to 5 days.

The Cowboy Way

I LEARNED ABOUT *The Code of the West* (also called Gene Autry's Cowboy Code, or the Cowboy Commandments) when we first moved to Wyoming. Its simplicity really moved me and it resonated because my dad has always loved the cowboy way of life. He actually paid his way through law school by singing country music in bars in Sun Valley, Idaho.

When I was little, my dad would quote country songs as wisdom. "You know, there's this old country song. It says . . ." As a kid, I'd roll my eyes, but now I value the lessons he shared. He believes country music is the only kind of music with something meaningful to say. He's old school like that. He gave me a book of Hank William's song lyrics when I was a little girl and I read it like it was poetry.

The Code of the West feels like it was written by my dad. He taught me to ski at Baldy Mountain when I was three years old, and he's the reason I love the mountains and chose to settle my family here. He always said, "If you're lucky enough to be in the mountains, you're lucky enough."

Everything you need to follow to live a solid, happy life is in those words.

THE CODE OF THE WEST
(Courtesy of the Center for Cowboy Ethics and Leadership)

1. Live each day with courage.
2. Take pride in your work.
3. Always finish what you start.
4. Do what has to be done.
5. Be tough, but fair.
6. When you make a promise, keep it.
7. Ride for the brand.
8. Talk less and say more.
9. Remember that some things aren't for sale.
10. Know where to draw the line.

Orange-Zested, Cardamom-Spiced Carrot Cake Cupcakes with Maple Cream Cheese Frosting

MAKES 12 CUPCAKES

FOR THE CUPCAKES

1¼ cups all-purpose flour

1 teaspoon baking powder

½ teaspoon baking soda

½ teaspoon kosher salt

1 teaspoon ground cinnamon

1 teaspoon ground cardamom

½ teaspoon ground ginger

½ cup oil (grapeseed, vegetable, or canola oil)

¼ cup granulated sugar

¾ cup packed dark brown sugar

2 large eggs, room temperature

⅓ cup unsweetened applesauce

1 teaspoon pure vanilla extract

1 cup grated carrots (about 2 large carrots)

½ cup toasted walnuts, finely chopped

½ cup golden raisins

1 tablespoon freshly grated orange zest

Oven-Dried Citrus, for garnish (see sidebar on page 84)

FOR THE MAPLE CREAM CHEESE FROSTING

½ cup unsalted butter, room temperature

8 ounces full-fat cream cheese, room temperature

3¼ cups confectioners' sugar, sifted

¼ cup cornstarch or buttermilk powder

¼ cup pure maple syrup

1 teaspoon pure vanilla extract

Pinch of kosher salt

Preheat the oven to 350 degrees F. Prepare the cupcake pan with paper liners. Set aside.

To make the cupcakes, in a large bowl, whisk together the flour, baking powder, baking soda, salt, cinnamon, cardamom, and ginger. Set aside.

In another bowl with a wooden spoon, mix the oil, sugars, eggs, applesauce, and vanilla until combined. No brown sugar lumps should be present. Pour the wet ingredients into the dry ingredients, and, using a wooden spoon, mix until completely combined. Stir in the carrots, chopped walnuts, raisins, and orange zest. The batter will be thick and chunky. Using an ice cream scoop or large spoon, fill each cupcake liner ⅔ full. Bake for 18 minutes, or until a tester inserted into the center of the cupcakes comes out

continued >

clean. Allow the cupcakes to cool in the pan for 5 minutes, then transfer to a wire rack to cool completely.

To make the frosting, in the bowl of an electric mixer on medium-high speed, beat the butter and cream cheese until light and fluffy, about 3 minutes. Add the confectioners' sugar, 1 cup at a time, mixing well after each addition. Add the cornstarch or buttermilk powder. Mix well. Add the maple syrup, vanilla extract, and salt. Mix on medium-high speed until smooth, about 2 minutes.

To assemble, top each cupcake with a generous swirl of cream cheese frosting. Decorate with oven-dried citrus.

NOTE: The swirl was made with an open star piping tip Ateco #828.

OVEN-DRIED CITRUS

1 blood orange
1 cara cara orange
1 navel orange

Preheat the oven to 200 degrees F. Line two baking sheets with parchment paper. With a sharp knife, slice the citrus about ¼ inch thick. Lay the slices in a single layer about 1 inch apart on the prepared baking sheets. Bake for 3 to 4 hours. Turn them over halfway through the baking time. Allow them to cool before using.

I added a pop of edible gold leaf to the dried citrus. Use a dry paint brush to apply. Edible gold leaf is sold in sheets and easily found in craft stores and online.

Pistachio-Amaretto Cupcakes with Raspberry Buttercream

MAKES 12 CUPCAKES

FOR THE CUPCAKES

- 1 heaping cup shelled pistachios
- 1¾ cups cake flour
- 1 teaspoon baking powder
- ¼ teaspoon baking soda
- ½ teaspoon kosher salt
- ½ cup unsalted butter, room temperature
- 1 cup granulated sugar
- 3 egg whites, room temperature
- 1 teaspoon pure vanilla extract
- ½ cup full-fat sour cream, room temperature
- ½ cup whole milk, room temperature
- ¼ cup Amaretto liqueur

FOR THE RASPBERRY BUTTERCREAM

- ¾ cup fresh raspberries
- 1½ cups unsalted butter, room temperature
- 4½ cups confectioners' sugar, sifted
- 3 tablespoons heavy cream
- 1 teaspoon pure vanilla extract
- Pinch of kosher salt

FOR ASSEMBLY

- Pistachio crumbs
- Fresh raspberries

Preheat the oven to 350 degrees F. Prepare a cupcake pan with paper liners. Set aside.

To make the cupcakes, in a food processor, grind the pistachios into fine crumbs. In a medium bowl, combine the pistachio crumbs, cake flour, baking powder, baking soda, and salt. Whisk to combine. Set aside.

In the bowl of an electric mixer on medium-high speed, cream the butter and sugar together until light and fluffy, about 3 minutes. Add half of the egg whites, mix well to combine. Add the remaining egg whites, mix well to combine. Add the vanilla and sour cream. Mix on medium speed until fully combined, scraping down the bowl if needed. With the mixer on low, add half the dry ingredients, followed by half the milk. Repeat with the remaining dry ingredients and milk. Mix until just combined. Slowly stir in the Amaretto until combined. Using an ice cream scoop or large spoon, fill each cupcake liner ⅔ way full. Bake for 18 to 20 minutes, or until

continued >

a tester inserted into the center of the cupcakes comes out clean.

Allow the cupcakes to cool in the pans for 5 minutes, then transfer to a wire rack to cool completely.

To make the buttercream, in a food processor, purée the raspberries until they're the texture of a smoothie. Put them through a mesh strainer to remove the seeds. Set aside.

In the bowl of an electric mixer on medium-high speed, cream the butter for about 3 minutes. The butter should lighten in color and become fluffy. Add the confectioners' sugar, 1 cup at a time, mixing well after each addition. Add the cream and mix well. Add the vanilla extract. With the mixer on low, add the purée by the spoonful, until the desired color and flavor is achieved. For me, it is about 4 to 5 tablespoons. Because the purée is juicy, you want to add a little at a time so the frosting doesn't get runny. If you add too much, add a little more confectioners' sugar. Add a pinch of salt. Mix the buttercream for another 2 minutes until light and fluffy.

To assemble the cupcakes, top each cupcake with a generous amount of raspberry buttercream. Garnish with pistachio crumbs and fresh raspberries.

NOTE: The buttercream flower was made with Wilton petal piping tip 123.

Fluffy Yellow Sheet Cake with Milk Chocolate Frosting

MAKES 1 (9 X 13-INCH) SHEET CAKE

FOR THE CAKE

2½ cups cake flour

2 teaspoons baking powder

¼ teaspoon baking soda

¾ teaspoon kosher salt

¾ cup unsalted butter, room temperature

1¾ cups granulated sugar

2 large eggs

1 large egg yolk

2½ teaspoons pure vanilla extract

1 cup buttermilk, room temperature

FOR THE MILK CHOCOLATE FROSTING

8 ounces high-quality milk chocolate, chopped

1 tablespoon light corn syrup

1 cup heavy cream

1 teaspoon pure vanilla extract

Pinch of kosher salt

American Buttercream flowers (see page 44 for recipe and page 33 for instructions) for decorating (optional)

Sprinkles (optional)

continued >

Preheat the oven to 350 degrees F. Butter a 9 x 13-inch cake pan. Line the bottom with parchment paper. Dust the interior of the pans generously with flour, then tip over to knock out the excess, leaving a thin coating.

To make the cake, in a medium bowl, sift together the cake flour, baking powder, baking soda, and salt. Set aside.

In a bowl of an electric mixer on medium speed, cream the butter and sugar together until light and fluffy, about 3 minutes. On low speed, add the eggs and egg yolk, 1 at a time, mixing well after each addition. Scrape down the bowl. Add the vanilla. Mix well, about 1 minute. On low speed, slowly add half of the dry ingredients, followed by half of the buttermilk. Scrape down the bowl. Repeat with the remaining dry ingredients and buttermilk. Mix until just combined. Pour the batter into the cake pan and spread into an even layer. Bake for 30 to 35 minutes, or until a

tester inserted into the center of the cake comes out clean. Set aside to cool on a wire rack for 10 minutes. Remove the cake from the pan and let it cool completely.

To make the frosting, in a heatproof bowl, add the chopped milk chocolate and corn syrup. In a medium saucepan, bring the cream to a simmer. Pour the cream over the chocolate and syrup and cover with aluminum foil. Let the chocolate mixture sit for 5 minutes. Remove the foil. Add the vanilla extract and a pinch of salt. Whisk until smooth. Cover and refrigerate for at least 1 hour until cooled and slightly firm. In the bowl of an electric mixer fitted with a paddle attachment on medium-high speed, beat the chocolate mixture until thick and creamy.

Using an offset spatula, spread the frosting evenly over the cooled cake. Decorate with buttercream flowers and sprinkles, if using.

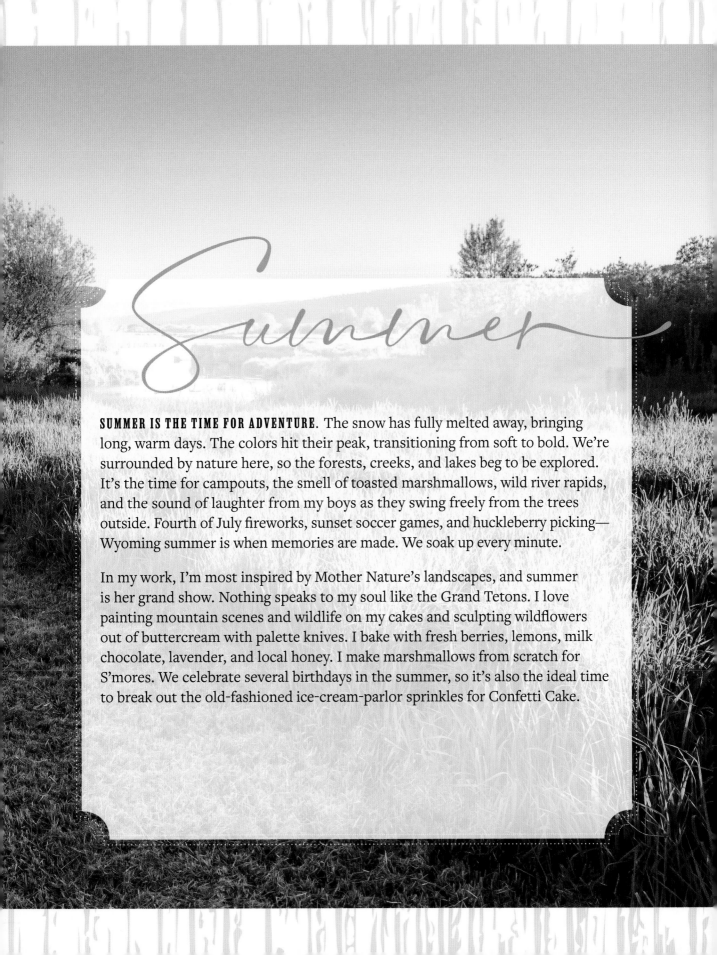

Summer

SUMMER IS THE TIME FOR ADVENTURE. The snow has fully melted away, bringing long, warm days. The colors hit their peak, transitioning from soft to bold. We're surrounded by nature here, so the forests, creeks, and lakes beg to be explored. It's the time for campouts, the smell of toasted marshmallows, wild river rapids, and the sound of laughter from my boys as they swing freely from the trees outside. Fourth of July fireworks, sunset soccer games, and huckleberry picking—Wyoming summer is when memories are made. We soak up every minute.

In my work, I'm most inspired by Mother Nature's landscapes, and summer is her grand show. Nothing speaks to my soul like the Grand Tetons. I love painting mountain scenes and wildlife on my cakes and sculpting wildflowers out of buttercream with palette knives. I bake with fresh berries, lemons, milk chocolate, lavender, and local honey. I make marshmallows from scratch for S'mores. We celebrate several birthdays in the summer, so it's also the ideal time to break out the old-fashioned ice-cream-parlor sprinkles for Confetti Cake.

THE DESSERT TABLE

ESTABLISH A MOOD

For the dessert buffet, I like to highlight my surroundings and bring those elements into my design. I usually lean toward an eclectic-farmhouse or rustic-elegance vibe. Wherever you are, starting with a theme will help you select your display pieces and featured desserts. You can take inspiration from your setting, the season, the invitation, or the celebratory occasion. I often get inspired by decorative objects, like a hand-painted antique dessert plate.

PICK THE RIGHT SURFACE

With imagination, any surface can be used for a dessert table. An old barn door laid across wine barrels, an antique dresser, a catering table dressed in linens, even the bed of a vintage pickup truck. Make sure the surface space fits the number of desserts you have. For a single cake, select a small table to showcase it. For a large spread, select a large round or rectangle table so your desserts won't be crowded. If the table can be accessed from multiple angles, make sure all desserts can be easily reached.

LOCATION, LOCATION, LOCATION

To enhance the beauty and photogenic appeal of your dessert table, create a backdrop. My favorite backdrop is the natural environment, often a mountain landscape or rustic barn, but when that isn't available, create something. This can be a floral arch, a wood panel draped with fabric, or charming signage.

STICK TO A COLOR AND TEXTURE PALETTE

Color and texture will set the stage for your table, allowing your desserts to tell the story. Within your palette, be creative, selecting colors and textures that will highlight your desserts. Soft dusty rose and muted pinks, lightly draped linens, peonies, and gold accents create bohemian romance. Rich woods, mismatched plates, galvanized tin, sage and ivory, wildflowers, and antlers suggest rustic woodland. Bright white porcelain, crisp navy and green, orchids, and clean lines evoke organic modern.

START WITH THE CENTERPIECE

Whether it's a single-tiered cake, a cupcake tower, or a collection of small cakes, start with the star of the table. I like this dessert to be the highest and placed in the center, then I arrange the other desserts at varying heights around it, much like a pyramid. On a longer table you may have two or three pyramids at play. If so, make sure your center pieces are well balanced along the table.

THINK OUTSIDE THE BOX

Use props and fillers to vary height and dimension; this creates visual interest and allows each dessert to make its own statement. I love to use a mix of cake stands, tiered dessert trays, wood pedestals, stacked plates, and trays to create layers of height and dimension. Add life to empty spaces with florals, greenery, or candlelight. Unique props can be found in unlikely places: a stack of old books to create height, or a row of glass kitchen canisters to hold cookies or macarons.

SOURCES FOR DISPLAY

Visit craft stores such as JoAnn's and Michael's, antique stores or flea markets, and eclectic boutiques like Anthropologie. Kitchen and home stores, like Pottery Barn, Williams-Sonoma, and Sur La Table, are rife with possibilities. Family heirlooms—maybe your mom's china collection, or unique pieces borrowed from friends—make for a one-of-a-kind display.

CHOOSE USER-FRIENDLY DESSERTS

A dessert table is a gathering station, for tasting and conversation. I like to keep things bite-size, wrapped in paper for ease of handling, and not too messy. Chances are your guests will grab more than one treat, so offer variety. Cupcakes, cookies, cookie sandwiches, bars, mini tarts, and mason-jar desserts are my favorites. Consider your environment and audience. Is there a local ingredient you'd like to highlight? Will there be children attending the event? To appeal to all tastes, combine light flavors, like vanilla, berry, and citrus, with darker flavors, like caramel, chocolate, and nut butters. Have napkins and stacks of plates in multiple locations. For an extra thoughtful touch, add to-go boxes so guests can take some desserts home.

Strawberry and Lavender Cake with Wildflower Honey Buttercream

MAKES 1 (3-LAYER 8-INCH) CAKE

FOR THE CAKE

- 1½ tablespoons dried culinary lavender
- 3⅔ cups cake flour
- 2 teaspoons baking powder
- ¾ teaspoons baking soda
- 1 teaspoon kosher salt
- ¾ cup unsalted butter, room temperature
- 2 cups granulated sugar
- 3 large eggs, room temperature
- 2 egg whites, room temperature
- 2 teaspoons pure vanilla extract
- 1½ cups buttermilk, room temperature

FOR THE STRAWBERRY SAUCE

- 1 pound fresh strawberries, quartered
- ¼ cup granulated sugar
- 2 teaspoons fresh lemon juice
- ½ teaspoon pure vanilla extract

WILDFLOWER HONEY BUTTERCREAM

- 1½ cups unsalted butter, room temperature
- 1 (8-ounce) block full-fat cream cheese, room temperature
- 5½ cups confectioners' sugar, sifted
- 1 teaspoon pure vanilla extract
- ¼ cup wildflower honey
- ¼ teaspoon kosher salt

Preheat the oven to 350 degrees F. Butter 3 (8-inch) cake pans and line the bottoms with parchment paper. Dust the interior of the pans generously with flour, then tip over to knock out the excess, leaving a thin coating. Set aside.

To make the cake, using a spice grinder or mortar and pestle, grind the lavender to a fine powder. Set aside. In a medium bowl, whisk together the flour, baking powder, baking soda, and salt. Set aside.

In the bowl of an electric mixer on medium speed, beat the butter for 1 minute to soften. Add the sugar and ground lavender. Mix on medium-high speed until light and fluffy, about 5 minutes. On low speed, add the eggs and egg whites, 1 at a time, mixing well after each addition. Add in the vanilla extract. Scrape down the bowl as needed.

On low speed, add one third of the dry ingredients, followed by half of the buttermilk. Mix until just combined. Add another third of the dry ingredients, followed by the remaining buttermilk. Mix until just combined. Add the remaining dry ingredients. Mix until just combined. Scrape down the bowl and give a final stir by hand.

continued >

Divide the batter evenly among the pre-pared cake pans. Bake on the center rack for 25 to 27 minutes, or until a tester inserted into the center of the cakes comes out clean. Allow the cakes to cool in their pans for 10 minutes before turn-ing over onto a wire rack. Allow them to cool completely before frosting.

To make the sauce, in a medium sauce-pan over medium heat, combine the strawberries, sugar, and lemon juice. Bring to a boil, stirring constantly, until the sugar fully dissolves. Simmer over medium-low heat, stirring occasionally, for 20 to 25 minutes until the strawber-ries have broken down and the sauce has thickened. Using a wooden spoon, gently crush the strawberries into the sauce. Stir in the vanilla extract. Pour the sauce into a heatproof bowl and allow to cool to room temperature, then cover and chill in the refrigerator for 1 hour. The sauce will thicken as it cools.

To make the buttercream, in the bowl of an electric mixer on medium-high speed, beat the butter until light and fluffy, 3 to 5 minutes. Add the cream cheese and mix for another minute. Mixing on low speed, add the confectioners' sugar, 1 cup at a time, mixing well after each addition. Scrape down the sides and bottom of the bowl. Add the vanilla extract, honey, and salt. Mix on medium speed for 3 minutes until the frosting is light and fluffy.

To assemble the cake, place 1 cooled cake layer, flat side facing down, on a cake plate or cake stand. Cover the top with a generous layer of buttercream. Add generous spoonfuls of strawberry sauce. Spread evenly over the top of the buttercream, leaving a 1-inch border around the cake edges. You don't want the sauce leaking out of the sides.

Place the second cake layer, flat side facing up, on top of the frosted first layer. Fill the gaps between the cake layers with buttercream. Repeat the steps with the buttercream and straw-berry sauce on the second layer.

Place the final cake layer, flat side facing up. Fill the gaps between the cake layers with buttercream. Cover the top and sides of the cake with a thin coat of buttercream to lock in the crumbs. Place in the refrigerator, uncovered, and chill for 15 minutes.

Remove cake from fridge and, with an offset spatula, apply a generous layer of buttercream frosting over the entire cake, starting at the top and smoothing down and over the sides.

NOTE: To decorate this cake, I used the palette knife technique and the textured technique. I colored the buttercream with Colour Mill tints in lavender, purple, sage green, olive green, and yellow. For the bottom tier, I layered sev-eral buttercream colors over each other, scrapping off areas to reveal the below colors. For the top tier, I used palette knives to paint the flowers.

Western Weddings

THE MAJORITY OF the weddings I cater are destination events. People travel from all over the country to get married in Jackson Hole. The draw is the Grand Teton mountains. Catch a glimpse of those jagged snowy peaks set against a crisp blue sky and you'll understand the fuss. They pull at your heartstrings like a symphony. Treacherous and wild, but breathtaking. It's a sight you'll never forget. And isn't that what a wedding is all about, making memories?

I'm lucky enough to work where others vacation, which comes with a unique benefit. Everyone is filled with such contagious joy and energy; I can't help but jump on board and rediscover this beautiful place all over again. The town of Jackson is like a living postcard. With its authentic western charm and rich history, it offers an experience unlike any other. It's home to two National Parks: Grand Teton and Yellowstone. It's a window into a world of wildlife you've only seen on National Geographic. The antler-arched town square is photo-ready from every angle. For lovers of the outdoors, it's paradise, filled with picturesque lakes, hiking trails, and scenic river floats. And the food is marvelous. The taste of Jackson Hole is something to write home about.

I love every element of a western wedding. The sprawling ranch venues, the creative minds of the event designers, the artisan florals, the custom paper goods, the caterers, and the photographers that capture it all. I enjoy and admire every vendor I'm lucky enough to work with. We've become friends and have built trust, tackling this wild, unpredictable landscape together. It can snow on a ceremony in mid-June, so you learn to expect the unexpected and adapt. No two weddings are the same and each, somehow, seems to be more beautiful than the last.

But for me, it's all about the cake.

Couples come to me to help them celebrate what makes this place so special. I try my best to capture this feeling through cake, making their wedding day artfully inspired. It may sound a bit touchy-feely, but I truly believe desserts are a love language, one we all live to speak. A celebration of two lives coming together; there's no better time to indulge.

The cake should be delicious *and* make a stunning statement. It can be done with flavors that capture the West, like the highly coveted wild huckleberry and local wildflower honey: vibrant and bright, bringing smiles to faces with the first bite. Or whiskey and caramel: rustic and cozy, like a flannel blanket keeping you warm on a crisp winter night. It can be inspired by a setting, like the dramatic Tetons at sunset, or the river when a cutthroat trout breaks the surface of the water. It can be done with natural elements, like native pressed wildflowers or foraged elk antlers.

However it manifests itself, the cake and desserts tell a story, the couple's story.

Whatever brought them to Wyoming, whatever they hope to take home, whatever they want for their future together, I strive to bring those feelings to life through edible art. The art may be short-lived, but the memory and photos live on forever. Forever West.

Buttermilk Vanilla Bean Cake with Huckleberry Jam and Vanilla Bean Buttercream

A classic vanilla cake with a Rocky Mountain twist, this is my most requested wedding cake flavor. I use a local huckleberry jam.

MAKES 1 (3-LAYER 8-INCH) CAKE

FOR THE CAKE

- 3 cups cake flour
- 2 teaspoons baking powder
- 1 teaspoon kosher salt
- 1 cup unsalted butter, room temperature
- ⅓ cup oil, canola, vegetable, or grapeseed
- 1¾ cups granulated sugar
- 4 extra large eggs, room temperature
- 2 extra large egg whites, room temperature
- 1 heaping tablespoon vanilla bean paste
- 1 cup buttermilk, room temperature

FOR THE VANILLA BEAN BUTTERCREAM

- 2 cups unsalted butter, room temperature
- 6 cups confectioners' sugar, sifted
- 3 teaspoons vanilla bean paste
- 4 tablespoons heavy cream, room temperature
- ¼ teaspoon kosher salt

FOR ASSEMBLY

- 1 (8-ounce) jar huckleberry jam

Preheat the oven to 350 degrees F. Butter 3 (8-inch) cake pans and line the bottoms with parchment paper. Dust the interior of the pans generously with flour, then tip over to knock out the excess, leaving a thin coating. Set aside.

To make the cake, in a medium bowl, whisk together the cake flour, baking powder, and salt. Set aside. In the bowl of an electric mixer on high speed, beat the butter, oil, and sugar until light and fluffy, 3 to 5 minutes. It should look slightly paler in color and have no lumps. On low speed, add the eggs and the egg whites, 1 at a time. Add the vanilla bean paste. Beat on medium speed, until fully combined. Scrape down the bowl as needed.

On low speed, add half of the dry ingredients to the butter mixture, mixing until fully combined. Then add half of the buttermilk, mixing until fully combined. Repeat with the remaining dry ingredients and remaining buttermilk, mixing until just combined. Scrape down

continued >

Add the vanilla bean paste, heavy cream, and salt. Mix on medium-high speed for about 3 minutes, until fluffy and smooth. Using a rubber spatula or wooden spoon, stir by hand to remove any air bubbles.

To assemble the cake, place 1 cooled cake layer, flat side facing down, on a cake plate or cake stand. Cover the top with a generous layer of buttercream. Add generous spoonfuls of huckleberry jam. Spread evenly over the top of the buttercream, leaving a 1-inch border around the cake edges. You don't want the jam leaking out of the sides.

Place the second cake layer, flat side facing up, on top of the frosted first layer. Fill the gaps between the cake layers with buttercream. Repeat the steps with the buttercream and huckleberry jam on the second layer.

Place the final cake layer, flat side facing up. Fill the gaps between the cake layers with buttercream. Cover the top and sides of the cake with a thin coat of buttercream to lock in the crumbs. Place in the refrigerator and chill, uncovered, for 15 minutes.

Remove the cake from fridge and, with an offset spatula, apply a generous layer of buttercream frosting over the entire cake, starting at the top and smoothing down and over the sides.

the bowl and finish mixing with a rubber spatula. Evenly divide the batter among the cake pans. Bake on the center rack for 20 to 25 minutes, or until a tester inserted into the center of the cakes comes out clean. Allow the cakes to cool in their pans for 10 minutes before turning over onto a wire rack. Allow them to cool completely before frosting.

To make the buttercream, in the bowl of an electric mixer on high speed, cream the butter on until light and smooth, about 5 minutes. Add the confectioners' sugar, 1 cup at a time, mixing well after each addition. Scrape down the bowl.

Dark Red Velvet Cake with Chocolate Ganache and Cream Cheese Frosting

Dark cocoa powder and chocolate ganache take red velvet cake to a whole new dark and silky level.

MAKES 1 (3-LAYER 8-INCH) CAKE

FOR THE CAKE

- 2¼ cups all-purpose flour
- 3 tablespoons dark Dutch-process cocoa powder, such as Hershey's Special Dark
- 1½ teaspoons baking soda
- ½ teaspoon kosher salt
- 1 cup buttermilk, room temperature
- 3 large eggs, room temperature
- 1 tablespoon pure vanilla extract
- 1 tablespoon distilled white vinegar
- ½ cup unsalted butter, room temperature
- ¼ cup oil, canola, vegetable, or grapeseed
- 1½ cups granulated sugar
- 2 tablespoons red food coloring or 1 to 2 teaspoons of red gel food coloring

Meringue cookies (optional)
Edible gold leaf (optional)

FOR THE CHOCOLATE GANACHE

- 1 cup high-quality dark chocolate, finely chopped
- ½ cup heavy cream

Pinch of kosher salt

FOR THE CREAM CHEESE FROSTING

- 1 cup unsalted butter, room temperature
- 16 ounces full-fat cream cheese, room temperature
- ½ cup buttermilk powder or cornstarch
- 6 cups confectioners' sugar, sifted
- 2 teaspoons pure vanilla extract
- ⅛ teaspoon kosher salt

Preheat the oven to 350 degrees F. Butter 3 (8-inch) cake pans and line the bottoms with parchment paper. Dust the interior of the pans generously with cocoa powder, then tip over to knock out the excess, leaving a thin coating. Set aside.

To make the cake, in a medium bowl, whisk together the flour, dark cocoa powder, baking soda, and salt. In another large bowl, whisk together the buttermilk, eggs, vanilla extract, and vinegar. Set aside.

continued >

In the bowl of an electric mixer on medium-high speed, beat the butter, oil, and sugar until light and fluffy, 3 minutes. On low speed add half of the dry ingredients. Mix to combine. Then add half of the buttermilk mixture. Mix to combine. Scrape down the bowl as needed. Repeat with the remaining dry ingredients and buttermilk mixture. Mix until just combined. Using a rubber spatula, stir in the red food coloring until evenly colored.

Divide the batter evenly among the prepared cake pans. Bake on the center rack for 25 minutes, or until a tester inserted into the center of the cakes comes out clean. Allow the cakes to cool in their pans for 10 minutes before turning over onto a wire rack. Allow them to cool completely before frosting.

To make the ganache, place the chopped chocolate in a heatproof bowl. In a medium saucepan over medium-high heat, bring the heavy cream to a simmer. Pour the simmering cream over the chocolate. Cover with aluminum foil and let it sit for 3 to 5 minutes. Whisk until smooth. Stir in a pinch of salt to taste. Let the ganache cool to room temperature. It will thicken as it sets. If necessary, reheat in the microwave for 10 to 15 seconds.

To make the frosting, in an electric mixer on medium-high speed, beat the butter and cream cheese together until combined, about 2 minutes. Add the buttermilk powder or cornstarch. Mix until combined. Add the confectioners' sugar, 1 cup at a time, mixing well after each addition. Add the vanilla extract and salt. Mix to combine. Beat the frosting for about 3 more minutes until it's smooth and fluffy.

To assemble the cake, place 1 cooled cake layer, flat side facing down, on a cake plate. Add a heaping ½ cup of cream cheese frosting to the top. Using an offset spatula, spread evenly to the edges. Spoon a generous layer of room-temperature ganache over the top, spreading almost to the edges, leaving a 1-inch border. Top with a second cake layer. Repeat with another layer of cream cheese frosting, spreading evenly to the edges. Add another layer of ganache on top, spreading almost to the edges, leaving a 1-inch border. Top with the final cake layer, flat side facing up. Spread the remaining frosting over the top. Using the offset spatula, add any remaining frosting to the sides of the cake to fill in gaps between layers. Then smooth to create a semi-naked finish. Decorate with meringue cookies and edible gold leaf if you wish.

Red, White, and Blue Meringue Cookies

MAKES ABOUT 24 COOKIES

Red and blue liquid food coloring or gel
   food coloring
4 large egg whites, room temperature
¼ teaspoon cream of tartar
⅛ teaspoon kosher salt
1 cup granulated sugar
1 teaspoon pure vanilla extract

Snip the tip off a 12- to 16-inch clear plastic piping bag. Insert a large open star piping tip firmly at the base of the bag. Using a food-safe paint brush, paint 2 to 3 wide vertical red stripes inside the bag, starting from the piping tip to the end of the bag. Don't worry about being too neat. The colors will blend together as you fill and pipe. Repeat with 2 to 3 blue stripes, leaving 2 to 3 open stripes of clear plastic in between each color; the meringue will be the white stripes. Set aside while you make the meringue.

Preheat the oven to 225 degrees F. Line two baking sheets with parchment paper or silicone mats.

In the bowl of an electric mixer fitted with the whisk attachment on high speed, beat the egg whites, cream of tartar, and salt until soft peaks form, 3 to 4 minutes. With the mixer on low speed, slowly add the sugar. Increase to high speed and beat until stiff peaks form, 2 to 3 minutes. Add the vanilla extract and beat until combined. The meringue should be thick and marshmallow-like. Working quickly, using a rubber spatula, fill the interior of the prepared piping bag. Pipe meringue dollops onto the baking sheets 2 inches apart.

Bake on the center rack for 60 minutes. Keeping the oven door closed, turn off the heat. Let the meringues cool in the oven for an additional 1 hour, until light and dried throughout. Remove from the oven and allow to cool completely before transferring to a wire rack. Store the cookies in an airtight container for up to 2 weeks.

NOTE: For these cookies, I used Ateco piping tip 849.

Lemon Drop Cupcakes

MAKES 12 TO 14 CUPCAKES

FOR THE CUPCAKES

1½ cups all-purpose flour

2 teaspoons baking powder

½ teaspoon kosher salt

1 heaping tablespoon freshly grated lemon zest

½ cup buttermilk, room temperature

¼ cup freshly squeezed lemon juice

1 teaspoon pure vanilla extract

½ cup unsalted butter, room temperature

1 cup granulated sugar

2 large eggs, room temperature

1½ cups Fresh Lemon Curd (page 129)

FOR THE VANILLA BUTTERCREAM

1 cup unsalted butter, room temperature

3 cups confectioners' sugar

1 teaspoon pure vanilla extract

2 tablespoons heavy cream, room temperature

Pinch of kosher salt

Preheat the oven to 350 degrees F. Prepare a cupcake pan with paper liners. Set aside.

To make the cupcakes, in a medium bowl, whisk together the flour, baking powder, salt, and lemon zest. Set aside. In a glass measuring cup, combine the buttermilk, lemon juice, and vanilla extract. Set aside.

In the bowl of an electric mixer on medium high speed, cream the butter and sugar together until light and fluffy, 3 minutes. On low speed, add the eggs, 1 at a time, mixing well after each addition. Scrape down the bowl as needed. On low speed, add half of the dry ingredients. Mix to combine. Then add half of the buttermilk mixture. Mix to combine. Scrape down the bowl as needed. Repeat with the remaining dry ingredients and buttermilk mixture. Mix for 30 seconds, until fully combined and smooth. Using an ice-cream scoop or large spoon, fill each cupcake liner ⅔ full. Bake for 18 to 19 minutes, or until a tester inserted into the center of the cupcakes comes out clean. Allow the cupcakes to cool in their pan for 5 minutes, then transfer to a wire rack to cool completely.

continued >

To make the buttercream, in the bowl of an electric mixer on high speed, cream the butter until light and smooth, about 5 minutes. Add the confectioners' sugar, 1 cup at a time, mixing well after each addition. Scrape down the bowl. Add the vanilla extract, heavy cream, and salt. Mix on medium-high speed for about 3 minutes, until fluffy and smooth. Using a rubber spatula or wooden spoon, stir by hand to remove any air bubbles.

To assemble the cupcakes, use a small paring knife or apple corer to scoop out the center of each cupcake. Fill the interior with a scoop of fresh lemon curd. Top each cupcake with a generous swirl of vanilla buttercream.

NOTE: I used Wilton piping tip 1M.

Huckleberry Crumble Bars with Citrus Glaze

MAKES 12 BARS

FOR THE SHORTBREAD CRUST

- 1 cup unsalted butter, room temperature
- ½ cup granulated sugar
- 2 teaspoons pure vanilla extract
- 2 cups plus 3 tablespoons all-purpose flour
- ½ teaspoon kosher salt

FOR THE CRUMBLE TOPPING

- ½ cup old-fashioned rolled oats
- ⅓ cup packed light-brown sugar
- ¼ cup all-purpose flour

Pinch of kosher salt

Freshly grated zest of 1 orange

- 4 tablespoons unsalted butter, chilled and diced

FOR THE FILLING

- 1 cup huckleberry jam
- 1 cup fresh huckleberries

FOR THE CITRUS GLAZE

- 1 cup confectioners' sugar, sifted
- 2 tablespoons whole milk
- 1 tablespoon fresh orange juice
- ½ teaspoon pure vanilla extract

continued >

Preheat the oven to 325 degrees F. Butter an 8 x 10-inch baking pan. Line the bottom with parchment paper overhanging on two opposite sides for easy lifting out.

To make the crust, in the bowl of an electric mixer on medium-high speed, beat the butter and sugar until light and fluffy, about 3 minutes. Scrape down the bowl as needed. Add the vanilla extract and mix until combined. With the mixer on low speed, add the flour. Mix until combined. Spread the mixture evenly over the bottom and slightly up the sides of the prepared pan, pressing firmly. Bake the crust for 15 to 20 minutes, until lightly browned. Let the pan sit on a wire rack while you prepare the crumble topping.

Increase the oven temperature to 350 degrees F.

To make the crumble topping, in a medium bowl, combine the oats, brown sugar, flour, salt, and orange zest. Using a pastry blender or clean fingers, cut in the chilled butter until the mixture resembles coarse crumbs. Set aside.

For the filling, spread the huckleberry jam over the warm shortbread crust. Sprinkle with fresh huckleberries. Sprinkle the crumble topping evenly over the top. Bake for 30 minutes or until the huckleberry filling is bubbling and the topping is lightly browned. Cool on a wire rack while you make the glaze.

To make the glaze, in a medium bowl, whisk the confectioners' sugar, milk, orange juice, and vanilla extract together until smooth. Drizzle generously over the crumble topping. When cooled completely, using the parchment paper, lift out and cut into twelve bars.

Huckleberry Picking

I'M YOUR HUCKLEBERRY . . .

Before the beloved western *Tombstone* and Val Kilmer's infamous line "I'm your huckleberry," I had never heard of the elusive mountain plant. Growing up in Southern California, huckleberries weren't a common thing. It was more of an avocado kind of place. I didn't even know what huckleberries looked like. But in the Rocky Mountains of Wyoming, huckleberries grow wild and they're a sought-after regional flavor. Huckleberry honey, huckleberry jam, huckleberry syrup, and my favorite, huckleberry ice cream. You could say they're the famous berries of the Wild West.

Huckleberries can be challenging to find, but they are absolutely delicious and well worth the effort. Similar to blueberries, huckleberries are small with larger seeds, and have a deep purple, reddish color, sometimes with a hint of dark blue. For a tiny berry, their taste packs a punch; tangy and tart, but with a sweet finish. You'll find huckleberries in the forests, along mountain slopes, and around lake edges anywhere between 3,000 to 11,000 feet in elevation. They ripen during the summer season and peak in August.

Aside from being used in sweets and treats, huckleberries are incredibly healthy. They're full of antioxidants, vitamin C, iron, and potassium and can boost immunities.

Beloved by local folks and grizzly bears alike, locations for huckleberry picking are secrets well kept. There is nothing better than fresh huckleberries picked directly from the source, not to mention the beauty of the surrounding scenery. But no one wants those hidden gems to become a tourist attraction. Living in Wyoming, I heard rumors of huckleberry picking but I could never find anyone to take me. Finally, after living here nearly seven years, a native Wyoming friend, whose name, coincidentally, is Forrest, shared his highly coveted secret picking spot. He was bribed with cookies, of course, but I know he enjoyed passing along his mountain traditions and teachings to my kids.

Now, I would never betray his trust and give up his picking location. It's become our secret to keep. But I can tell you we were in the Grand Tetons and there were no people for miles. I will also tell you huckleberry picking comes with three rules:

1) No berry left behind. Pick the bush until it's empty.

2) You must delegate at least 30 seconds to recover a dropped berry.

3) You can only eat one handful of berries per hour of picking.

Soren, my youngest, ignored Forrest's rules, running excitedly from bush to bush, dropping many slippery berries, and then eating every single berry he picked on site. We came home with Tupperware containers full of huckleberries, and Soren came home with a belly ache and a smile on his face. When we got home I made the most delicious huckleberry pancakes, and we set a new summer tradition for our family. It was a good day. I now understand what the huckleberry fuss is all about.

Huckleberries are a key ingredient in many of my desserts. My vanilla cake layered with huckleberry jam, which I buy locally, is one of my most requested wedding cake flavors. Huckleberries can also be found at local farmers' markets. But if you're able, I highly recommend putting on some hiking books and hunting for your own secret spot. Or bribe a local with some delicious cookies. It's worth the effort.

Peanut Butter Swirl Fudge Brownies

MAKES 16 BROWNIES

FOR THE PEANUT BUTTER FILLING

½ cup smooth peanut butter

2 tablespoons unsalted butter, at room temperature

¼ cup confectioners' sugar

FOR THE BROWNIE LAYER

4 ounces high-quality semisweet chocolate, chopped

4 ounces high-quality unsweetened chocolate, chopped

½ cup unsalted butter

3 tablespoons unsweetened cocoa powder

1¼ cups granulated sugar

3 large eggs, room temperature

1 tablespoon pure vanilla extract

¾ teaspoon salt

1 cup all-purpose flour

Roasted, salted peanuts, chocolate chips, and flaked sea salt, for garnish

Preheat the oven to 350 degrees F. Butter and flour an 8 x 8-inch pan. Line the bottom with parchment paper leaving a 1-inch overhang on the sides.

To make the filling, in a medium bowl, whisk together the peanut butter, butter, and confectioners' sugar. Mix until smooth. Set aside.

To make the brownie layer, place the chocolates and butter in a heatproof bowl set over a pot filled with 1 inch of simmering water. Using a rubber spatula, stir until melted and smooth. Stir in the cocoa powder. Set aside to cool slightly.

In a large bowl, whisk together the sugar, eggs, vanilla extract, and salt. Using a rubber spatula, stir in the flour until fully combined. Pour half the batter into the prepared pan. Drop spoonfuls of half of the peanut butter mixture over the top, using a toothpick or butter knife to swirl it into the batter. Top with the remaining batter. Drop the remaining peanut butter mixture over the top, using a toothpick or butter knife to swirl it into the batter. Bake for 35 to 40 minutes, or until a toothpick inserted comes out with a few crumbs. Remove from the oven and allow to cool in the pan on a wire rack for 2 hours. While still warm, top with peanuts, chocolate chips, and flaked sea salt. Once cooled, remove from the pan using the parchment paper handles, and cut into bars. Store in an airtight container in the refrigerator for up to 1 week.

Confetti Birthday Cake with Sour Cream-Vanilla Buttercream

MAKES 1 (3-LAYER 8-INCH) CAKE

FOR THE CAKE

- 3 cups all-purpose flour
- 1 tablespoon baking powder
- ¼ teaspoon baking soda
- 1 teaspoon kosher salt
- 1 cup unsalted butter, room temperature
- 2 cups granulated sugar
- 4 eggs, room temperature
- 1 tablespoon pure vanilla extract
- 1 cup buttermilk, room temperature
- ¾ cup rainbow sprinkles, plus extra for sprinkling

SOUR CREAM-VANILLA BUTTERCREAM

- 2 cups unsalted butter, room temperature
- 6 cups confectioners' sugar
- ½ cup sour cream, room temperature
- 2 teaspoons pure vanilla extract

Pinch of kosher salt

Preheat the oven to 350 degrees F. Butter 3 (8-inch) cake pans and line the bottoms with parchment paper. Dust the interior of the pans generously with flour, then tip over to knock out the excess, leaving a thin coating. Set aside.

To make the cake, in a medium bowl, whisk together the flour, baking powder, baking soda, and salt. Set aside.

In the bowl of an electric mixer on medium-high speed, cream the butter and sugar together until light and fluffy, 3 minutes. Add the eggs, 1 at a time, mixing well after each addition. Add the vanilla extract. Scrape down the bowl as needed. With the mixer on low speed, slowly add the dry ingredients. Mix until combined. Continue mixing on slow speed to add the buttermilk. Mix until just combined. With a rubber spatula, give the batter a stir by hand, scraping up from the bottom. Gently fold in ¾ cup rainbow sprinkles.

Divide the batter evenly among the prepared cake pans. Bake on the center rack for 22 to 25 minutes, or until a tester inserted into the center of the cakes comes out clean. Allow the cakes to cool in their pans for 10 minutes before turning over onto a wire rack. Allow them to cool completely before frosting.

continued >

To make the buttercream, in a medium bowl with an electric mixer on high speed, cream the butter until light and smooth, 3 to 5 minutes. Add the confectioners' sugar, 1 cup at a time, mixing well after each addition. Scrape down the bowl. Add the sour cream, vanilla extract, and salt. Mix on medium-high speed for 3 minutes, until fluffy and smooth. Using a rubber spatula or wooden spoon, stir by hand to remove any air bubbles.

To assemble the cake, place 1 cooled cake layer, flat side facing down, on a cake plate or cake stand. Cover the top with a generous layer of buttercream, spreading evenly to the cake edges. Sprinkle a small handful of sprinkles over the top. Place the second cake layer, flat side facing up, on top of the frosted first layer. Cover the top with a generous layer of buttercream, spreading evenly to the cake edges. Sprinkle a small handful of sprinkles on top. Place the final cake layer, flat side facing up. Fill the gaps between the cake layers with buttercream. Cover the top and sides of the cake with a thin coat of buttercream to lock in the crumbs. Refrigerate, uncovered, for 15 minutes. Remove the cake from the fridge and, with an offset spatula, apply a generous layer of buttercream frosting over the entire cake, starting at the top and smoothing down and over the sides. Refrigerate for another 15 to 20 minutes before decorating.

NOTES: For the cake drip, I used the Roxy & Rich Cake Drip in Pale Blue. It's a quick and simple ready-made product; just heat up the bottle and drip away. The orange stars are made from Wilton candy melts. The painted "sprinkle" exterior is done with food coloring and a food safe paint brush. Painting on a cake must be done when the buttercream is chilled. Piping was done with Wilton tip 1M.

Blackberry-Buttermilk Pie with Vanilla Whipped Cream

MAKES 1 (9-INCH) PIE

FOR THE CRUST

2½ cups all-purpose flour

1 tablespoon granulated sugar

1 teaspoon kosher salt

8 tablespoons unsalted butter, well chilled and cut into cubes

8 tablespoons vegetable shortening, well chilled and cut into cubes

½ cup ice water, plus a few table-spoons more if needed

1 tablespoon apple cider vinegar

Heavy cream for brushing

Coarse sugar for sprinkling

BLACKBERRY-BUTTERMILK FILLING

2 heaping cups fresh blackberries, plus more for garnish

1 tablespoon fresh lemon zest

2 teaspoons fresh lemon juice

½ cup unsalted butter, melted and cooled

1½ cups granulated sugar

4 large eggs, room temperature

1 cup buttermilk, room temperature

3 tablespoons fine stone-ground yellow cornmeal

2 teaspoons pure vanilla extract

¼ teaspoon freshly grated nutmeg

¼ teaspoon ground cloves

¼ teaspoon kosher salt

VANILLA WHIPPED CREAM

1 cup heavy cream, very cold

1 tablespoon granulated sugar

1 teaspoon vanilla bean paste

¼ teaspoon freshly grated nutmeg

Dried flowers, for garnish

To make the crust, in a large bowl, mix the flour, sugar, and salt. Add the cubed butter and shortening. With a pastry blender, blend until the mixture begins to resemble small peas. Mix the vinegar into the ice water. Drizzle a few tablespoons of water over the flour-and-butter mixture and mix with a fork. Add more water until the dough begins to come together. Once the dough becomes moist and clumps together, it's hydrated enough. Divide the dough into 2 balls. Flatten them into disks and wrap in plastic wrap. Refrigerate for 1 hour.

Remove 1 disk of dough from the refrigerator 30 minutes before you're ready to use so it will roll out easily. Save the second disk for another use. Roll out the disk of dough on a well-floured surface to a 12-inch circle. The dough should be larger than your pie dish. Carefully transfer the dough to your pie dish. (I fold

continued >

the dough over my rolling pin to make it easy.) Gently press the dough into the sides of the dish leaving 1 inch of overhang on the sides. Fold the overhanging dough over the top and crimp the sides together. Refrigerate while you prepare your filling.

To make the filling, in a food processor, purée the blackberries, lemon zest, and lemon juice until they're the texture of a smoothie. Put them through a mesh strainer to remove the seeds. You should have about ¾ cup of purée.

Preheat the oven to 350 degrees F.

In a food processor, blend together ½ cup of the blackberry purée (you will have a little bit leftover), melted butter, sugar, eggs, buttermilk, cornmeal, vanilla extract, nutmeg, cloves, and salt. Mix until well combined. Pour the filling into the prepared pie crust. Brush the pie crust edges with the heavy cream and sprinkle generously with sugar. Bake on the center rack for 30 minutes. Reduce the temperature to 325 degrees F. Bake

for an additional 30 to 40 minutes or until the filling is set around the edges but there's still a slight wobble in the center. Allow the pie to cool on a wire rack for 2 hours before serving so it sets.

To make the whipped cream, for best results, chill the metal bowl of the electric mixer for 20 minutes ahead of time. Using the whisk attachment, add the heavy cream to the chilled bowl. Beat on medium-high speed until soft peaks form. Add the sugar, vanilla bean paste, and nutmeg. Continue beating for 20 to 30 seconds more until stiff peaks form. Be careful to not over beat. Serve immediately.

Serve the pie with a generous dollop of whipped cream and decorate with fresh blackberries and dried flowers.

NOTE: The crust dough will keep in the fridge, tightly wrapped in plastic, for 1 week, and will keep frozen for 1 month. I like using a larger recipe so I have the option of making a second pie.

Strawberry-Lemon Cookie Sandwiches

MAKES 24 (3-INCH) COOKIE SANDWICHES

FOR THE COOKIES

- 2¾ cups all-purpose flour plus extra for rolling out the dough
- ⅓ cup cornstarch
- ¾ teaspoon kosher salt
- 1 tablespoon freshly grated lemon zest
- 1 cup unsalted butter, room temperature
- 4 ounces full-fat cream cheese, room temperature
- 1 cup granulated sugar
- 1 extra large egg yolk, room temperature
- 1 teaspoon pure vanilla extract
- 2 tablespoons fresh lemon juice

FOR THE STRAWBERRY FILLING

- 1 cup freeze-dried strawberries
- 1 cup unsalted butter, room temperature
- 3 cups confectioners' sugar, sifted, plus more for dusting
- 1 teaspoon pure vanilla extract
- 3 tablespoons heavy cream

Pinch of kosher salt

½ to ¾ cup Fresh Lemon Curd (page 129)

To make the cookies, in a medium bowl, whisk together the flour, cornstarch, salt, and lemon zest. Set aside.

In the bowl of an electric mixer on medium-high speed, cream the butter, cream cheese, and sugar together until combined, 1 to 2 minutes. Add the egg yolk, vanilla extract, and lemon juice. Mix until fully combined. Scrape down the bowl as needed. With the mixer on low speed, add the flour mixture. Continue mixing on medium-low speed until the dough comes together. Wrap the dough in plastic wrap and refrigerate for 30 to 60 minutes.

Preheat the oven to 375 degrees F. Line two baking sheets with parchment paper.

On a well-floured surface, roll the dough out to about ¼ inch thick. Cut into desired shapes with cookie cutters of choice. Using a spatula, transfer the dough to the prepared baking sheets, placing them 2 inches apart. Bake for 12 to 13 minutes, until firm and crisp around the edges. Allow the cookies to cool for 5 minutes on the baking sheet before transferring them to a wire rack to cool completely.

To make the filling, using a food processor or blender, process the freeze-dried strawberries to a powdery dust. You

continued >

don't want any small pieces remaining. You will have roughly ½ cup. Set aside.

In the bowl of an electric mixer on high speed, cream the butter for 2 to 3 minutes, until light and fluffy. Add the confectioners' sugar and mix until well combined. Scrape down the bowl. Add the vanilla extract, heavy cream, and pinch of salt. Mix until combined. Add the freeze-dried strawberry powder. Mix on medium-high speed for 2 minutes, until light and fluffy. Spoon the filling into a pastry bag with the tip cut off.

To assemble the cookies, pipe a thick border of strawberry filling around the interior of a cookie. Using a small spoon, fill the center of the border with a dollop of lemon curd, being careful not to over-fill. Firmly press another cookie on top.

Refrigerate the cookies, covered, for 30 minutes to firm up the filling. Just before serving, dust with confectioners' sugar. Cookies will keep in an airtight container in the refrigerator for 1 week.

Fresh Lemon Curd

MAKES ABOUT 1½ CUPS

- 2 **extra large egg yolks**
- 1 **extra large egg**
- ¾ **cup granulated sugar**
- ⅓ **cup fresh lemon juice**
- 1 **tablespoon freshly grated lemon zest**
- 6 **tablespoons unsalted butter, diced, room temperature**
- ½ **teaspoon pure vanilla extract**

Pinch of kosher salt

In a medium saucepan over medium heat, whisk together the egg yolks, egg, sugar, lemon juice, and lemon zest until smooth. Continue whisking constantly to prevent the eggs from curdling for 5 to 7 minutes, until a thermometer registers 160 degrees F, and the curd is thick enough to coat the back of a spoon.

Remove from the heat and whisk in the butter, vanilla extract, and pinch of salt.

Place a fine-mesh sieve over a heatproof bowl. Using a rubber spatula, push the curd through the sieve to catch any curdling that may have occurred while cooking. Cover the curd with plastic wrap, touching the top layer of the curd, to prevent a film from forming. Chill overnight.

Happy Trails Cookies

When I was a little girl my dad would take us backpacking in Idaho. I was the youngest and the slowest. My dad would use trail mix to bribe me to keep moving on the trail. Of course, I only ate the M&Ms. These cookies are my new hiking motivation.

MAKES 18 TO 20 LARGE COOKIES

1½ cups all-purpose flour

1¼ cups old-fashioned rolled oats

1 teaspoon baking soda

½ teaspoon kosher salt

1½ cups unsalted butter, room temperature

¾ cup packed brown sugar

½ cup granulated sugar

1 large egg, room temperature

1 teaspoon pure vanilla extract

¾ cup peanut butter, chunky or smooth

1 cup pretzels or peanut-butter-filled pretzels, chopped into chunks

1 cup M&Ms

1 cup semisweet chocolate chips

Flaked sea salt

In a large bowl, whisk together the flour, oats, baking soda, and salt. Set aside.

In the bowl of an electric mixer on medium-high speed, beat the butter and sugars until light and fluffy, about 3 minutes. Add the egg and vanilla extract. Mix to combine. Scrape down the bowl as needed. Add the peanut butter. Mix to combine. With the mixer on low speed, add the dry ingredients. Mix until just combined. With a rubber spatula or wooden spoon, stir in the pretzels, M&Ms, and chocolate chips. Cover the dough and refrigerate for at least 3 hours or overnight.

Preheat the oven to 350 degrees F. Line two baking sheets with parchment paper.

Using an ice-cream scoop, scoop up the dough and place on the baking sheets 2 inches apart. Bake for 12 to 13 minutes, until lightly browned on the edges. Remove from the oven and sprinkle with flaked sea salt. Let the cookies cool on the baking sheet for 5 minutes, then transfer to a wire rack to cool completely.

Homemade Salted Caramel Marshmallows

MAKES 20 MARSHMALLOWS

Confectioners' sugar for dusting
1 cup cold water, divided
3 packets unflavored gelatin
1½ cups granulated sugar
1 cup light corn syrup
Heaping ¼ teaspoon kosher salt
1 tablespoon pure vanilla extract
½ cup Salted Caramel Sauce
(page 78), warmed to a
pourable consistency
Flaked sea salt

Line an 8 x 10-inch baking dish with parchment paper, leaving an overhang on opposite sides, to allow for easy lift out. Generously dust the bottom with confectioners' sugar. Set aside.

In the bowl of an electric mixer fitted with the whisk attachment, mix ½ cup of cold water with the gelatin. Allow the gelatin to sit and fully dissolve while you make the syrup.

In a medium saucepan, combine the remaining ½ cup water, sugar, corn syrup, and salt. Cook over medium heat, stirring, until the sugar dissolves. Turn the heat to high, and cook until the syrup reaches 240 degrees F on a candy thermometer. Remove from the heat. With the mixer on low speed, carefully pour the hot sugar mixture into the dissolved gelatin. Mix to combine. Turn the mixer

to high speed. Mix for 15 minutes until fluffy and very thick. The mixture will be room temperature.

Working quickly, drizzle salted caramel sauce over the bottom of the prepared baking dish. Sprinkle with flaked sea salt. Pour half of the marshmallow mixture over the salted caramel. Using a buttered spatula, spread to the edges of the dish. Drizzle more caramel sauce over the top. Sprinkle with flaked sea salt. Add the remaining marshmallow mixture over the top and spread evenly to the edges of the dish. Drizzle with caramel sauce and a sprinkle of flaked sea salt. Dust the top with confectioners' sugar.

Let the marshmallows sit uncovered overnight, until fully dry. Turn them over onto a confectioners' sugar–dusted board and cut into squares with a sharp knife. Store the marshmallows in an airtight container at room temperature for up to 1 week.

NOTES: For a vanilla bean marshmallow, omit the caramel sauce and flaked sea salt. Substitute 2 tablespoons vanilla bean paste for vanilla extract.

For a confetti marshmallow, omit the caramel sauce and flaked sea salt. With the vanilla, stir in ½ cup rainbow sprinkles.

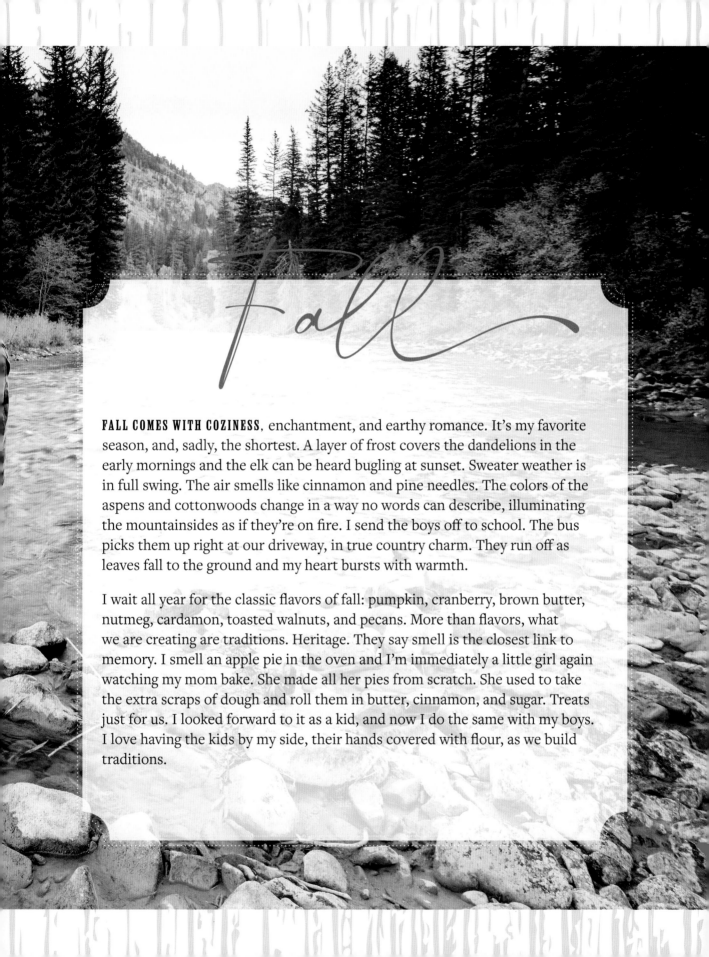

Fall

FALL COMES WITH COZINESS, enchantment, and earthy romance. It's my favorite season, and, sadly, the shortest. A layer of frost covers the dandelions in the early mornings and the elk can be heard bugling at sunset. Sweater weather is in full swing. The air smells like cinnamon and pine needles. The colors of the aspens and cottonwoods change in a way no words can describe, illuminating the mountainsides as if they're on fire. I send the boys off to school. The bus picks them up right at our driveway, in true country charm. They run off as leaves fall to the ground and my heart bursts with warmth.

I wait all year for the classic flavors of fall: pumpkin, cranberry, brown butter, nutmeg, cardamon, toasted walnuts, and pecans. More than flavors, what we are creating are traditions. Heritage. They say smell is the closest link to memory. I smell an apple pie in the oven and I'm immediately a little girl again watching my mom bake. She made all her pies from scratch. She used to take the extra scraps of dough and roll them in butter, cinnamon, and sugar. Treats just for us. I looked forward to it as a kid, and now I do the same with my boys. I love having the kids by my side, their hands covered with flour, as we build traditions.

MAGIC INGREDIENTS

BAKING IS A CRAFT. The finished product is a treat. My perspective is, if you're going to indulge, you should do it right. Taking baking to the next level is all about that magic ingredient. Looking beyond the basics of flour, sugar, and leaveners, I keep some specialty items on hand that are game changers for almost any recipe.

BLACK COCOA POWDER

Ultra smooth and the darkest of dark, black cocoa powder is a highly processed form of cocoa powder. It's ultra-Dutch processed to reduce acidity, which gives it a very deep chocolate flavor, similar to an Oreo cookie. Because the flavor is so deep, I like to mix only a few tablespoons of black cocoa with my regular cocoa to enhance the chocolate flavor in my desserts. It's essential in my homemade chocolate sandwich cookies (page 180). Black cocoa can be a challenge to find, but a little goes a long way. I usually purchase it online.

BOOZE

But just a little. Bourbon whiskey is my go-to for most desserts. It's versatile and warms the tummy. I also enjoy a touch of spiced rum, Grand Marnier, Amaretto, and Chambord. From cake to fruit fillings, a touch of liquor or liqueur adds depth and richness, enhancing the ingredients you're baking with. I add it to buttercream, salted caramel sauce, fresh berries, and many of my cakes and cupcakes.

BROWN BUTTER

Who doesn't love butter? But brown butter? That takes the cake. Brown butter (see page 76) is exactly what it sounds like: butter melted and lightly browned on the stovetop. The flavor is toasty, nutty, and all kinds of delicious. I add brown butter to my chocolate chip cookies, blondies, and my buttercream.

BUTTERMILK POWDER

I'm a big cream cheese frosting fan, but its soft texture makes it a challenge for stacking and decorating cakes. Buttermilk powder is my magic fix. When added along with confectioners' sugar, it thickens the consistency and makes it more stable. It also adds a rich, tangy flavor to complement the sweet frosting.

CORNSTARCH

Cornstarch is tasteless and creates a soft, tender crumb when added to shortbread, cookies, cream cheese frosting, and cut-out sugar cookies. Cornstarch is also used to thicken pie fillings and sauces.

FLAKED SEA SALT

When I want to finish a dessert, like freshly baked chocolate cookies, I love to use flaked sea salt. It provides a clean, pure flavor that provides the perfect contrast to sweet. It has a beautiful white color that pops against dark chocolate. It really shines in dessert sauces, like salted caramel and chocolate ganache.

FRESH CITRUS ZEST

The zest of citrus fruits carries intense flavors. They're filled with concentrated natural oils that will take your bakes and buttercreams to a new dimension. I add lemon zest to my sugar cookies, short-bread crusts, buttercreams, and cakes.

FRESHLY GRATED NUTMEG

When grated fresh, nutmeg adds a bright, bold, and nutty flavor to baked dishes. It's the magic ingredient to my Old-Fashioned Snickerdoodles (page 75), pies, and Bourbon Banana Cake with Bourbon Cream Cheese Buttercream (page 177).

GROUND ESPRESSO POWDER

If I'm baking with chocolate, I'm adding ground espresso powder. Coffee and chocolate are best friends. A teaspoon of espresso powder enhances the chocolate flavor of cakes, brownies, buttercreams, and ganaches without creating a coffee dessert. Of course, if you want coffee flavor, there's no better way to achieve it than ground espresso powder. Just add more.

HIGH-QUALITY CHOCOLATE

Be better than cheap chocolate. Using high-quality chocolate results in a difference you'll taste. Plus, it's better for you. Good chocolate contains less sugar and milk and high levels of cocoa. The fewer ingredients listed, the better. Look for 70-percent cocoa or more. It should also have a clean, sharp snap when it breaks.

KOSHER SALT

I tossed out harsh, bitter table salt many moons ago. Kosher salt is my go-to for just about everything. It's a flat-grained salt with no additives, so it's gentle and mild. Kosher salt enhances the flavor of your food; it doesn't overpower it. From baking to cooking to finishing, it's a staple in my pantry.

VANILLA BEAN PASTE

Vanilla bean paste is a blend of vanilla beans and concentrated vanilla. With a thicker consistency and specks of vanilla bean, the flavor is more intense than pure vanilla extract. Vanilla bean paste can be more costly, sometimes only found at specialty grocery stores or online, so I use it sparingly, when I want the vanilla flavor to shine, like in my Vanilla Whipped Cream (page 124).

Peanut Butter and Chocolate Oreo Cake

MAKES 1 (6-LAYER 8-INCH) CAKE

FOR THE CAKE

2¼ cups all-purpose flour

3 teaspoons baking powder

¾ teaspoon baking soda

1 teaspoon kosher salt

¾ cup unsalted butter

1¼ cups Dutch-processed cocoa powder

2 teaspoons espresso powder

1½ cups hot water

1½ cups buttermilk, room temperature

1½ cups packed light brown sugar

1½ cups granulated sugar

3 large eggs, room temperature

2 teaspoons pure vanilla extract

½ teaspoon almond extract

FOR THE PEANUT BUTTER-OREO BUTTERCREAM

2 cups unsalted butter, room temperature

1¼ cups smooth peanut butter

6 cups confectioners' sugar, sifted

¼ cup heavy cream

1 tablespoon pure vanilla extract

¼ teaspoon kosher salt

¼ cup finely ground Oreo crumbs, center filling removed

FOR ASSEMBLY

1½ cups crushed Peanut Butter Oreos

Preheat the oven to 350 degrees F. Butter 3 (8-inch) cake pans and line the bottoms with parchment paper. Dust the interior of the pans generously with cocoa powder, then tip over to knock out the excess, leaving a thin coating. Set aside.

To make the cake, in a large bowl, whisk together the flour, baking powder, baking soda, and salt. Set aside. In a medium saucepan over medium heat, melt the butter. Add the cocoa powder and espresso powder. Stir until smooth. Set aside to cool slightly.

In the bowl of an electric mixer on medium speed, combine the cocoa-butter mixture, hot water, buttermilk, and sugars. Mix until smooth. Add the eggs, 1 at a time, mixing well after each addition. Add the vanilla and almond extracts. Mix until combined. With the mixer on low speed, add the flour mixture. Mix for 60 seconds until no flour lumps remain.

Divide the batter evenly among the prepared cake pans. Bake for 30 to 35 minutes or until a tester inserted into the center of the cakes comes out clean.

continued >

Allow the cakes to cool in the pans for 10 minutes before turning over onto a wire rack. Allow them to cool completely before frosting.

To make the buttercream, in the bowl of an electric mixer on medium-high speed, beat the butter until light and fluffy, about 3 minutes. Add the peanut butter and mix until combined. Scrape down the bowl. Add the confectioners' sugar, 1 cup at a time, mixing for about 30 seconds after each addition. Add the heavy cream, vanilla extract, and salt. Mix until combined. On medium speed, mix for 3 minutes until light and fluffy. With a rubber spatula, stir in the Oreo crumbs.

To assemble the cake, with a serrated knife or cake leveler, divide each cake layer horizontally, making two thin cake layers, and six cake layers in all.

Place 1 cooled cake layer, flat side facing down, on a cake plate. Add a heaping ¼ cup of buttercream to the top. Using an offset spatula, spread evenly to the edges. Sprinkle with crushed Peanut Butter Oreos. Repeat with four layers of cake, buttercream, and crushed Oreos.

Top with the final cake layer, flat side facing up. Using an offset spatula, add a thin layer of buttercream to the top and sides of the cake to fill in gaps between layers. Then smooth to create a semi-naked finish. Sprinkle the top with crushed Peanut Butter Oreos.

NOTE: For the photograph on page 138, I sliced the cake layers horizontally with a cake leveler. This created multiple layers, giving the cake a more dramatic look when sliced. Follow the instructions for assembly, but repeat the steps to accommodate the extra layers. Be sure to add less buttercream between the layers so you don't run out.

To decorate this cake, I made the trees from sugar cones. I tinted the buttercream with Colour Mill forest green. Using a palette knife, I added dollops of buttercream to the outside of the cones, creating branches. Refrigerate the cones on a baking sheet for 15 minutes until firm. Dust them lightly with confectioners' sugar to create a snow-like effect. For the cake exterior, after frosting, I added Oreo cookie crumbs to the sides, here and there, to create a birch bark effect.

Apple Spice Cake with White Chocolate Ganache and Cinnamon-Cream Cheese Frosting

MAKES 1 (3-LAYER 6-INCH) CAKE

FOR THE CAKE

2¼ cups all-purpose flour

1 tablespoon ground cinnamon

1 teaspoon ground cardamom

½ teaspoon ground allspice

½ teaspoon ground cloves

¼ teaspoon freshly ground nutmeg

½ teaspoon kosher salt

½ teaspoon baking soda

½ teaspoon baking powder

1 cup unsalted butter, room temperature

1 cup packed brown sugar

¾ cup granulated sugar

2 large eggs, room temperature

3 large egg yolks, room temperature

1 tablespoon pure vanilla extract

1 cup buttermilk, room temperature

1 cup grated apples, such as Granny Smith

Dried apple chips for decorating

FOR THE WHITE CHOCOLATE GANACHE

1 cup finely chopped high-quality white chocolate

⅓ cup heavy cream

CINNAMON-CREAM CHEESE FROSTING

1½ cups unsalted butter, room temperature

8 ounces full-fat cream cheese, room temperature

5½ cups confectioners' sugar, sifted

2 teaspoons pure vanilla extract

1½ teaspoons ground roasted cinnamon such as McCormick Gourmet

Pinch of kosher salt

Preheat the oven to 350 degrees F. Butter 3 (6-inch) cake pans and line the bottoms with parchment paper. Dust the interior of the pans generously with flour, then tip over to knock out the excess, leaving a thin coating. Set aside.

To make the cake, in a medium bowl, whisk together the flour, cinnamon, cardamom, allspice, cloves, nutmeg, salt, baking soda, and baking powder. Set aside.

In the bowl of an electric mixer on medium-high speed, cream the butter and sugars together on until light and fluffy, about 3 minutes. Scrape down the bowl. Add the eggs and egg yolks, 1 at a time. Mix well after each addition. Add in the vanilla extract. Scrape down the bowl as needed.

On low speed, add one third of the dry ingredients, followed by half of the buttermilk. Mix until just combined. Add another third of the dry ingredients, followed by the remaining buttermilk.

continued >

Mix until just combined. Add the last of the dry ingredients. Mix until just combined. Scrape down the bowl. With a rubber spatula, stir in the grated apples. The batter will be thick. Divide the batter evenly among the prepared cake pans.

Bake on the center rack for 30 to 35 minutes, or until a tester inserted into the center of the cakes comes out clean.

Allow the cakes to cool in the pans for 10 minutes before turning over onto a wire rack. Allow them to cool completely before frosting.

To make the ganache, place the chopped white chocolate in a heatproof bowl. In a medium saucepan over low heat, bring the heavy cream to a simmer. Pour the simmering cream over the white chocolate. Cover with aluminum foil and let it sit for 3 minutes. Whisk until smooth.

The ganache will thicken as it sits. Allow it to cool to room temperature before adding it to the cake. Reheat if necessary for a spreadable consistency.

To make the cream cheese frosting, in the bowl of an electric mixer on medium-high speed, cream together the butter and the cream cheese until light and fluffy, about 3 minutes. Add the confectioners' sugar, 1 cup at a time, mixing for about 30 seconds after each addition. Add the vanilla extract, cinnamon, and salt. Mix until combined. On medium speed, mix for 3 minutes until light and fluffy.

To assemble the cake, place 1 cooled cake layer, flat side facing down, on a cake plate or cake stand. Cover the top with a generous layer of cinnamon buttercream. Add a spoonful of room temperature (not warm) ganache, leaving a 1-inch border around the cake edges. You don't want the ganache leaking out of the sides. Place the second cake layer, flat side facing up, on top of the frosted first layer. Fill the gaps between the cake layers with buttercream. Repeat the steps with the buttercream and ganache. Fill the gaps between the cake layers with buttercream. Place the final cake layer, flat side facing up. Cover the top and sides of the cake with a thin coat of buttercream to lock in the crumbs. Refrigerate for 15 minutes, uncovered. Remove the cake from the fridge and, with an offset spatula, apply a generous layer of buttercream frosting over the entire cake, starting at the top and smoothing down and over the sides. Decorate with buttercream leaves and apple chips.

NOTES: I created my buttercream leaves using a palette knife. The buttercream is tinted with AmeriColor food gels in Forest Green, Sage, and Bright White. I added a highlight to the leaves with a copper-luster dust applied with a food-safe paintbrush. Apple chips can be found at your local grocery store.

Barn Animals

I'VE ALWAYS WANTED to have barn animals. They don't come inside, they don't sit on the couch watching TV with us, but they have unique personalities and are part of the family. Right now we have eleven chickens, six goats, and three pigs, McQueen, Bruno, and Fernando. Trouble, the sweetest Jersey cow, is the newest addition to our menagerie. The kids always name them. Turbo, Bob—you just never know what mood the boys will be in.

Raising them has been so special and has taught our kids that when you take care of your animals they give back to you. It gives the boys a foundation for life. They have chores they have to do to take care of them, they nurture and love them, and the animals give back in a way that's different from dogs and cats.

We love having our own eggs—it doesn't get more organic than that! It's true farm-to-table; seeing the hens eating bugs and pulling worms out of the ground illustrates this really cool cycle. The eggs taste incredible and are so different from the ones you buy at the grocery store. And we don't have to rely on purchased groceries.

Actually, we'll get so many eggs in spring and summer we'll give them away. It's so fun to gift them to people; then others can enjoy the experience too. And with so many eggs, we have to get creative: I'll make deviled eggs, egg salad, lemon curd, and cakes—though I do have to be careful with a really white cake because these yolks are so vibrant in color, they'll turn a vanilla cake orange.

We've gone through four cycles of goat births and we intend to start milking Lucy and make cheese as soon as she stops nursing the babies. Goat milk is nutritious and delicious, but having these animals is an obligation. It's not like you can slack off. It's work and you have to make it a priority.

Living with farm animals helps us feel connected to why we're here and what we're doing. It teaches humility and character. Sometimes nature has other plans; our ducks didn't survive the winter. But being close to nature teaches you the good lessons, and the hard lessons too. Even though they're painful, they're important to learn. They're life lessons. We look after the animals, and they in turn look after us.

Midnight Cake

MAKES 1 (3-LAYER 8-INCH) CAKE

FOR THE CAKE

- 1½ cups all-purpose flour
- 1 teaspoon baking soda
- ½ teaspoon baking powder
- ¾ teaspoon kosher salt
- ¼ cup Dutch-processed cocoa powder
- ¼ cup black cocoa powder (see page 136)
- 2 teaspoons espresso powder
- 4 ounces finely chopped bittersweet chocolate
- 1¼ cups boiling water
- 10 tablespoons unsalted butter, room temperature
- 1 cup packed brown sugar
- ½ cup granulated sugar
- 3 large eggs, room temperature
- ½ cup sour cream, room temperature
- 1 tablespoon pure vanilla extract

FOR THE MIDNIGHT BUTTERCREAM

- 2 cups unsalted butter, room temperature
- ½ cup Dutch-processed cocoa powder
- ½ cup black cocoa powder
- 5 cups confectioners' sugar
- 5 tablespoons heavy cream
- 1 tablespoon pure vanilla extract
- ¼ teaspoon kosher salt

Preheat the oven to 350 degrees F. Butter 3 (8-inch) cake pans and line the bottoms with parchment paper. Dust the interior of the pans generously with cocoa powder, then tip over to knock out the excess, leaving a thin coating. Set aside.

To make the cake, in a medium bowl, whisk together the flour, baking soda, baking powder, and salt. Set aside. In another bowl, combine the cocoa powders, espresso powder, and bittersweet chocolate. Slowly add the boiling water and whisk until smooth. Set aside to cool slightly.

In the bowl of an electric mixer on medium-high speed, beat the butter and sugars until light and fluffy, about 3 minutes. Add the eggs, 1 at a time, mixing well after each addition. Scrape down the bowl. Add the sour cream and vanilla extract. Mix until combined. On low speed, add half of the dry ingredients, followed by half of the chocolate mixture. Mix until just combined. Add the remaining dry ingredients, followed by the remaining chocolate mixture. Mix until just combined.

continued >

Divide the batter evenly among the prepared cake pans. Bake for 20 to 25 minutes or until a tester inserted into the center of the cakes comes out clean. Allow the cakes to cool in the pans for 10 minutes before turning over onto a wire rack. Allow them to cool completely before frosting.

To make the buttercream, in the bowl of an electric mixer on medium-high speed, beat the butter until light and fluffy. About 3 minutes. Add the cocoa powders and mix until combined. Scrape down the bowl. Add the confectioners' sugar, 1 cup at a time, mixing for about 30 seconds after each addition. Add the heavy cream, vanilla extract, and salt. Mix until combined. On medium speed, beat for 3 minutes until light and fluffy.

To assemble the cake, place 1 cooled cake layer, flat side facing down, on a cake plate. Add a heaping ½ cup of buttercream to the top. Using an offset spatula, spread evenly to the edges. Top with a second cake layer. Repeat with another layer of buttercream, spreading evenly to the edges. Top with the final cake layer, flat side facing up. Spread another ½ cup of the frosting over the top. Using the offset spatula, add a thin layer of buttercream to the top and sides of the cake to fill in gaps between layers. Then smooth to create a crumb coat. Refrigerate the cake for 15 minutes. Apply the remaining buttercream over the top and sides of the cake.

NOTES: To paint the pumpkin, I used edible gold luster dust. You mix a dime-size amount of dust with a drop or two of vodka to make a thick paste. Apply the "paint" with a food-safe brush. The vodka evaporates, leaving the gold behind. Make sure the buttercream is firm and chilled before adding painted details. Luster dusts can be found at local craft stores or online.

Bourbon Pumpkin Cheesecake

MAKES 1 (10-INCH) CHEESECAKE

FOR THE GRAHAM CRACKER PECAN CRUST

- ½ cup unsalted butter, melted, divided
- 2 heaping cups finely ground graham cracker crumbs
- ¾ cup toasted and finely chopped pecans
- ¼ teaspoon fine sea salt

FOR THE BOURBON PUMPKIN FILLING

- 3 (8-ounce) blocks full-fat cream cheese, room temperature
- 5 large eggs, room temperature, lightly beaten
- 1½ cups packed dark brown sugar
- 1 tablespoon vanilla bean paste
- 1 teaspoon ground cinnamon
- ½ teaspoon ground ginger
- ½ teaspoon ground cloves
- ¼ teaspoon freshly ground nutmeg
- ½ cup high-quality bourbon
- 1 (15-ounce) can pumpkin purée

FOR THE BAKED GRAHAM CRACKER CRUMBLE

- ½ cup graham cracker crumbs
- ¼ cup granulated sugar
- ¼ teaspoon baking powder
- ¼ teaspoon fine sea salt
- 2 tablespoons melted butter
- 1 teaspoon pure vanilla extract

BOURBON CREAM TOPPING

- 2 cups sour cream, room temperature
- ¼ cup high-quality bourbon
- ⅓ cup granulated sugar
- 1 teaspoon pure vanilla extract

continued >

Preheat the oven to 375 degrees F. Using 1 tablespoon of the melted butter, butter the sides and bottom of 1 (10-inch) springform pan.

To make the crust, in a medium bowl, mix the graham cracker crumbs, pecans and salt. Add the remaining butter and mix until evenly combined and moistened. Press the mixture firmly to cover the bottom of the pan and halfway up the sides. Place the springform pan on a baking sheet and bake on the center rack for 8 to 10 minutes, until set and golden brown. Let the crust cool on a wire rack. Lower the oven temperature to 350 degrees F.

To make the filling, in the bowl of an electric mixer on medium-high speed, beat the cream cheese until light and fluffy, about 3 minutes. Add the lightly beaten eggs, brown sugar, vanilla bean paste, cinnamon, ginger, cloves, and nutmeg. Mix until smooth. With the mixer on low speed, add the bourbon. Mix until combined. Add the pumpkin purée. Mix until fully combined, about 2 minutes. Scrape down the bowl as needed.

Pour the batter onto the prepared crust. Bake for 60 minutes, until the sides are set and the center is slightly jiggly. Keeping the cheesecake in the oven with the door slightly ajar, turn the oven off and let the cake sit for another 60 minutes, allowing the cheesecake to set completely. Once cooled and set, cover and refrigerate for several hours or overnight.

Preheat the oven to 300 degrees F. Line a baking sheet with parchment paper.

To make the crumble, in a medium bowl, mix the graham cracker crumbs, sugar, baking powder, and salt together until combined. Add the butter and vanilla extract. Mix together until clumps form. Spread the mixture onto the parchment paper in an even layer. Bake for 13 to 15 minutes until crisp and golden brown. Allow the crumbles to cool completely.

To make the cream topping, preheat the oven to 400 degrees F. In a medium bowl, whisk the sour cream, bourbon, sugar, and vanilla together until smooth. Pour the topping in an even layer over the top of the cheesecake. Bake for 10 minutes. Do not let the topping brown, you simply want it to set. Allow the cheesecake to cool on a wire rack. Pile the crumbles generously on top of the cheesecake before serving.

NOTE: This cheesecake can be made several days ahead, kept covered, and refrigerated.

Sweater-Weather Pumpkin-Oatmeal Cookies

MAKES 24 COOKIES

2 cups all-purpose flour

1 teaspoon baking soda

1½ teaspoons pumpkin pie spice

1½ teaspoons ground cinnamon

¼ teaspoon freshly ground nutmeg

1 teaspoon kosher salt

¾ cup unsalted butter, room temperature

1 cup packed dark brown sugar

⅓ cup granulated sugar

1 tablespoon unsulfured molasses

1 large egg, room temperature

1 tablespoon pure vanilla extract

⅔ cup pumpkin purée

1½ cups old-fashioned rolled oats

8 ounces high-quality white baking chocolate, chopped into chunks

1 cup toasted chopped pecans

In a medium bowl, whisk the flour, baking soda, pumpkin pie spice, cinnamon, nutmeg, and salt until well mixed. Set aside. With an electric mixer on medium-high speed, cream the butter, sugars, and molasses until light and fluffy, about 3 minutes. Scrape down the bowl as needed.

On low speed, add the egg and vanilla extract. Mix until well combined. Add the pumpkin. Mix until well combined. Slowly add the flour mixture. Mix until just combined. Scrape down the bowl as needed. With a wooden spoon, stir in the oats, white chocolate chunks, and pecans. Cover and refrigerate for at least 2 hours or overnight.

Preheat the oven to 350 degrees F. Line two baking sheets with parchment paper.

With an ice cream scoop, drop the dough onto the prepared baking sheets, spacing about 2 inches apart. Bake for 13 to 15 minutes until lightly browned on the edges. Allow the cookies to cool for 10 minutes on the baking sheets, then transfer to a wire rack to cool completely.

Cookies will keep in an airtight container at room temperature for 5 days.

Spiced Sugar Cookies

MAKES ABOUT 24 (3-INCH) COOKIES

2½ cups all-purpose flour

1 teaspoon kosher salt

1 teaspoon ground cinnamon

½ teaspoon ground ginger

¼ teaspoon freshly grated nutmeg

¼ teaspoon ground allspice

⅛ teaspoon ground cloves

1 cup unsalted butter, room temperature

1 cup packed light brown sugar

1 large egg, room temperature

1 egg yolk

1 tablespoon pure vanilla extract

Confectioners' Sugar Glaze (page 156) or Vanilla Buttercream (page 111), for decorating

In a medium bowl, sift together the flour, salt, cinnamon, ginger, nutmeg, allspice, and cloves. Set aside.

In the bowl of an electric mixer on medium speed, cream together the butter and brown sugar until light and fluffy, about 3 minutes. Add the egg and egg yolk, 1 at a time. Mix well after each addition. Add in the vanilla extract. Scrape down the bowl when needed. With the mixer on low speed, slowly add the flour mixture. Mix until just combined.

Divide the dough in half and flatten into disks. Wrap each disk separately in plastic wrap. Refrigerate for at least 2 hours or overnight.

Preheat the oven to 375 degrees F. Line two baking sheets with parchment paper.

On a well-floured surface, roll the dough to ¼ inch thick. Use your favorite cookie cutters to cut the dough into shapes and place on the prepared baking sheets, leaving an inch or so between cookies. Bake on the center rack for 11 to 12 minutes, until lightly browned around the edges. Repeat with the remaining dough. Allow the cookies to cool for 10 minutes on the baking sheet, then transfer to a wire rack to cool completely. Decorate as desired using the glaze or buttercream.

These cookies will keep in an airtight container at room temperature for 2 weeks.

NOTES: These cookies taste delicious with a simple confectioners' sugar glaze or decorated with vanilla buttercream. To create the design on these cookies I used vanilla buttercream applied with a palette knife. The buttercream is tinted with AmeriColor food gels in chocolate brown, warm brown, ivory, forest green, and leaf green.

continued >

Confectioners' Sugar Glaze

MAKES ABOUT 1 CUP

1 cup confectioners' sugar, sifted
5 to 6 tablespoons whole milk
½ teaspoon pure vanilla extract

In a small bowl, mix the confectioners' sugar, 5 tablespoons milk, and vanilla together. Add another tablespoon of milk if needed to reach drizzling consistency. Use immediately to decorate cooled cookies or keep covered until ready to use. The glaze takes about an hour to harden and set.

Cardamom and Walnut Oatmeal Cream Pie Cookies with Brown Buttercream

MAKES 24 COOKIE SANDWICHES

FOR THE COOKIES

- 1½ cups all-purpose flour
- 1 teaspoon baking soda
- 1½ teaspoons ground cardamom
- ½ teaspoon ground cinnamon
- 1 teaspoon kosher salt
- 1 cup unsalted butter, room temperature
- ¾ cup packed dark brown sugar
- ½ cup granulated sugar
- 2 eggs, room temperature
- 1 tablespoon pure vanilla extract
- 3 cups old-fashioned rolled oats
- ¾ cup walnuts, toasted and finely chopped

FOR THE BROWN BUTTER BUTTERCREAM FILLING

- ½ cup solid brown butter (see page 76), room temperature
- 1¾ cups confectioners 'sugar
- ½ teaspoon pure vanilla extract
- 2 tablespoons heavy cream, room temperature

Pinch of kosher salt

Pinch of freshly grated nutmeg

To make the cookies, in a medium bowl, whisk together the flour, baking soda, cardamom, cinnamon, and salt. Set aside.

continued >

In the bowl of an electric mixer on medium-high speed, cream the butter and sugars until light and fluffy, 3 to 5 minutes. Add the eggs, 1 at a time. Add the vanilla extract. Mix well after each addition. Scrape down the bowl as needed. On slow speed, add the flour mixture. Mix until just combined. Scrape down the bowl as needed. Stir in the oats and walnuts. Cover the cookie dough and refrigerate for at least 2 hours. Don't skip this step, it helps keep the cookies from spreading in your oven.

Preheat the oven to 350 degrees F. Line two baking sheets with parchment paper.

Working with 1 tablespoon of dough at a time, drop the dough onto the prepared baking sheets, 2 inches apart. Bake for 10 to 12 minutes, until lightly browned on the outside. Allow the cookies to cool for 5 minutes on the baking sheets, then transfer them to a wire rack to cool completely.

To make the buttercream, in a medium bowl with an electric mixer on high speed, cream the butter until light and fluffy, about 2 minutes. Add the confectioners' sugar. Mix to combine. Add the vanilla extract, heavy cream, salt, and nutmeg. Mix on medium-high speed for about 3 minutes, until fluffy and smooth.

Using a rubber spatula or wooden spoon, stir the buttercream by hand to remove any air bubbles.

Spoon the filling into a pastry bag with the tip cut off. You can also use a butter knife or spoon for the filling if you like a more rustic look.

To assemble the cookies, swirl the filling over the top of one cookie and firmly press another cookie on top, being careful not to break it. Refrigerate the cookies, covered, for about 30 minutes to firm up the filling.

Store the cookies in an airtight container, kept chilled, for 1 week.

Repurposing Found Objects

JACKKNIFE CREEK RANCH dates back to 1930 when it was a working creamery and farm, and as a result, we have a cluster of barns on our land. Some are still standing, but some have fallen down and are just piles of barnwood. We've left them there because it's so authentic and the wood is so beautifully distressed and genuine. All these barns have history and a story that they tell. Back in the day they served a real purpose. They've been standing—without much structural integrity—and have lasted through winters and windstorms and time.

When my husband, Jeremiah, built the bakery for me, I wanted open shelving. He walked out to where the main barn had fallen down and realized he could use these hundred-year-old planks. We brought them back into our home and now they're in my bakery and they're one of my favorite things in that room. They have a purpose and are used every day. They're part of the history of the land and now they're part of my story.

There's also a shed outside with all these barn doors. We don't know where they came from or what they were used for, but they're obviously very old. They're incredible; they look like they've come from some architectural salvage field. Being that these wood pieces are so huge and we don't have anywhere to use them as doors, Jeremiah cut them down so I could use them for staging, photography, and as dessert boards for events. They have these rubbed-off finishes and wonderful texture; they're incredible. We took something that someone else might find useless and made them beautiful again.

I love repurposed things. It's never really something I'd thought about before, being in California; we never had the space we have here and we also never had pieces of history we could pull from and make new again. But I love this idea of one man's trash being another man's treasure. Rather than looking at something as junk, I think, how can I find another purpose for you?

We thought about using a door and turning it into a headboard for our bed, or we might lean it against the wall as an accent piece. Salvage yards are good sources for cool old things you can repurpose.

Junkyards are too, and old antique shops. Estate sales can be a great place to find stuff, as long as the items are authentic. I've seen people take vintage sofas, remove the cushions and make planters. Once I saw an old Victorian settee filled with succulents. Another way you can use junk as a planter is farmhouse sinks. If you do it right it can be amazing.

Jeremiah found an antique Ford truck bed on someone else's ranch; it was basically free. He thought he would bring this home and use it to tow firewood. He also thought, "My wife's going to kill me." But when he brought it home, I saw its old Wyoming plates and its rusted-over sides and that perfect blue, and I said, "This is amazing!" I wanted to make it into a flower bed and, rather than hide it, I wanted to make it a focal point of our yard. The next Mother's Day I found my husband and boys had turned it into a truck garden for me. Now every time I see it, I think, where have you been? Who had you? How did you end up here?

It's really about using your creativity. If you get any vibe from an object that it's special in some way, snatch it up, hang onto it, and wait for that lightbulb moment to make something out of it. The possibilities are endless.

Nutella Chocolate Chip Cookies

MAKES 24 COOKIES

3 cups all-purpose flour

2 teaspoons cornstarch

1¼ teaspoons baking soda

¼ teaspoon freshly grated nutmeg

¾ teaspoon kosher salt

¾ cup unsalted butter, room temperature

¾ cup packed light brown sugar

½ cup granulated sugar

2 large eggs, room temperature

1 tablespoon pure vanilla extract

½ cup Nutella

1 cup high-quality dark chocolate chips

½ cup toasted chopped hazelnuts

Flaked sea salt for sprinkling

Preheat the oven to 350 degrees F. Line two baking sheets with parchment paper.

In a medium bowl, whisk together the flour, cornstarch, baking soda, nutmeg, and salt. Set aside.

In the bowl of an electric mixer on medium-high speed, cream the butter and sugars until light and fluffy, about 3 minutes. Add the eggs, 1 at a time, and vanilla extract. Mix well after each addition. Scrape down the bowl. With the mixer on low speed, slowly add the dry ingredients. Mix until just combined. Add the Nutella by the spoonful until it's just incorporated, mixing for only 5 seconds. It should be streaked throughout the dough and not fully blended in. With a rubber spatula or wooden spoon, stir in the chocolate chips and hazelnuts. Be careful not to lose those streaks of Nutella!

Working with 2 tablespoons of dough at a time, drop them onto the prepared baking sheets, about 2 inches apart. Bake for 12 to 14 minutes until lightly browned on the edges. Remove from the oven and sprinkle with flaked sea salt. Allow the cookies to cool for 10 minutes on the baking sheets, then transfer to a wire rack to cool completely.

Cookies will keep in an airtight container at room temperature for 5 days.

NOTES: Depending on your oven, the natural oils in the Nutella may cause the cookies to spread. I keep a dinner spoon handy to gently push the edges in, keeping the cookies nice and round. This must be done immediately after removing the cookies from the oven.

Honey-Roasted Peanut Butter and Jelly Bars

MAKES 18 BARS

2 cups all-purpose flour

1 teaspoon baking powder

1 teaspoon kosher salt

¾ cup unsalted butter, room temperature

1 cup packed light brown sugar

⅓ cup granulated sugar

2 tablespoons honey

2 large eggs, room temperature

1 tablespoon vanilla extract

1 heaping cup peanut butter of choice

¾ cup honey-roasted peanuts, chopped

1 heaping cup high-quality strawberry jam

Preheat the oven to 350 degrees F. Butter and flour an 8 x 10-inch baking pan. Line the bottom with parchment paper leaving a 1-inch overhang on the sides.

In a medium bowl, whisk together the flour, baking powder, and salt. Set aside.

In the bowl of an electric mixer on medium speed, cream together the butter, sugars, and honey until light and fluffy, about 3 minutes. Add the eggs, 1 at a time, and vanilla, mixing well after each addition. Scrape down the bowl as needed. Add the peanut butter and mix to combine. With the mixer on low speed, slowly add the dry ingredients. Mix until just combined. With a rubber spatula or wooden spoon, stir in the chopped honey-roasted peanuts.

Set aside 1 cup of the cookie dough for the topping. Spread the rest of the dough in an even layer into the bottom of the prepared pan. Bake for 20 minutes, until golden brown around the edges. Let the pan cool to warm on a wire rack. Spread the strawberry jam over the crust in an even layer. Drop the remaining dough over the top by the spoonful, leaving some of the jam exposed. Bake for 45 minutes until the jam is bubbling and the topping is a golden brown.

Let the bars cool completely on a wire rack. Lift them from the pan and cut them into bars. The bars will keep for 3 to 5 days in an airtight container at room temperature.

Pumpkin Spice Latte Cupcakes

MAKES 12 CUPCAKES

FOR THE CUPCAKES

- 1 cup all-purpose flour
- 1 teaspoon ground cinnamon
- ½ teaspoon ground ginger
- ⅛ teaspoon ground allspice
- ¼ teaspoon freshly grated nutmeg
- ½ teaspoon kosher salt
- 1 teaspoon baking powder
- ½ teaspoon baking soda
- 2 large eggs, room temperature
- 1 teaspoon pure vanilla extract
- ¾ cup pumpkin purée
- ½ cup granulated sugar
- ¼ cup packed dark brown sugar
- ½ cup canola or vegetable oil

FOR THE CHOCOLATE-ESPRESSO AND CREAM CHEESE BUTTERCREAM

- 1 cup unsalted butter, room temperature
- 8 ounces full-fat cream cheese, room temperature
- ⅔ cup Dutch-process cocoa powder, sifted
- 1 teaspoon espresso powder
- 3½ cups confectioners' sugar, sifted

- 2 tablespoons heavy cream
- 1 teaspoon pure vanilla extract
- ⅛ teaspoon kosher salt
- ½ cup Salted Caramel Sauce (page 78) for drizzling, room temperature
- Chopped dark chocolate espresso beans for garnish

Preheat the oven to 350 degrees F. Line a cupcake tin with paper liners. Set aside.

To make the cupcakes, in a medium bowl, whisk together the flour, cinnamon, ginger, allspice, nutmeg, salt, baking powder, and baking soda. In another bowl, whisk together the eggs, vanilla, pumpkin, sugars, and oil. Using a rubber spatula or wooden spoon, add the dry ingredients to the pumpkin mixture. Mix to fully combine.

Using an ice cream scoop, fill the cupcake liners ⅔ full. Bake for 18 to 19 minutes or until a tester inserted into the center of the cupcakes comes out clean. Allow the cupcakes to cool in the pan for

continued >

5 minutes, then transfer to a wire rack to cool completely.

To make the buttercream, in the bowl of an electric mixer on medium-high speed, cream the butter and cream cheese until light and fluffy, about 3 minutes. Add the cocoa powder and espresso powder and mix until combined. Add the confectioners' sugar, 1 cup at a time, mixing well after each addition. Add the heavy cream, vanilla extract, and salt. Mix for another 3 minutes until light and fluffy.

Apply a generous swirl of the buttercream to each cupcake and top with a drizzle of salted caramel and espresso beans.

NOTE: The buttercream swirl was made with Wilton piping tip 1M.

Cranberry, Apple, and Walnut Pie

MAKES 1 (9-INCH) DOUBLE-CRUST PIE

FOR THE CRUST

2½ cups all-purpose flour

1 tablespoon granulated sugar

1 teaspoon fine sea salt

8 tablespoons unsalted butter, well chilled and cut into cubes

8 tablespoons vegetable shortening, well chilled and cut into cubes

½ cup ice water, plus a few table-spoons more if needed

1 tablespoon apple cider vinegar

Heavy cream for brushing

Coarse sugar for sprinkling

FOR THE FILLING

4 medium Granny Smith apples, peeled and sliced ¼ inch thick (roughly 8 cups)

1½ cups fresh cranberries

½ cup toasted walnuts, finely chopped

¾ cup granulated sugar

½ cup all-purpose flour

½ teaspoon kosher salt

1½ teaspoons ground cinnamon

½ teaspoon ground cardamom

¼ teaspoon freshly grated nutmeg

½ teaspoon ground allspice

1 tablespoon apple cider vinegar

1 tablespoon freshly grated orange zest

2 tablespoons Grand Marnier

1 tablespoon unsalted butter, diced

To make the crust, in a large bowl, mix the flour, sugar, and sea salt. Add the cubed butter and shortening. With a pastry blender, blend until the mixture begins to resemble small peas.

Mix the vinegar into the ice water. Drizzle a few tablespoons of water over the flour and butter mixture and mix with a fork. Add more water until the dough becomes moist and clumps together.

Divide the dough into two balls. Flatten them into disks and wrap in plastic wrap. Refrigerate for 1 hour. Remove the dough 30 minutes before you're ready to use so it will roll out easily. Dough will keep in the refrigerator, tightly wrapped in plastic wrap, for 1 week, and will keep frozen for 1 month.

continued >

Preheat the oven to 425 degrees F.

Roll out one disk of dough on a well-floured surface to a 12-inch circle. The dough should be larger than your 9-inch pie dish. Carefully transfer the dough to the pie dish. I fold the dough over my rolling pin to make it easy. Gently press the dough into the sides of the dish, leaving about an inch of overhang on the sides. Refrigerate while you prepare the filling.

To make the filling, in a large bowl, mix the apples, cranberries, walnuts, sugar, flour, salt, cinnamon, cardamom, nutmeg, allspice, vinegar, orange zest, and Grand Marnier. Pour the filling and juices into the prepared pie crust. Spread the pieces of diced butter over the top. Refrigerate while you roll out the top crust.

Roll out the other disk of dough to a circle. You can either keep the disk whole and place it over the top of the filling, or slice it into strips for a decorative lattice pie crust. Cover the top of the pie with the dough. If keeping the disk whole, cut 4 to 5 slits in the top to vent. Fold the overhanging dough over the top and crimp the sides together.

Brush the top with heavy cream and sprinkle generously with sugar. Bake the pie for 25 minutes. Lower the temperature to 375 degrees F. Bake for about 35 minutes more until the crust is golden brown and the filling is bubbling. Allow the pie to cool on a wire rack for about 5 hours before serving.

NOTE: This pie is delicious served slightly warm with vanilla bean ice cream.

Winter

WINTER TRULY IS A WONDERLAND. That first snowfall is pure magic. It begins as a dusting and soon becomes a heavy velvet blanket of white as far as the eye can see, turning the mountains into majestic ice castles. The days grow shorter and things become quiet. Families and friends come together for the holidays, sugar cookies cover my counter tops, and the fire is constantly roaring. The cold is intense; you feel it in your bones. We ski and sled, ending the day snuggled up in cozy flannel PJs and homemade hot cocoa. My favorite winter tradition is cutting down our own Christmas tree and watching the boys decorate it with handmade ornaments, their cheeks rosy and their eyes filled with wonder.

Baking is my love language and winter is my time to share it. A warm oven filled with cookies leads to a warm heart filled with comfort and joy. I dress the house with rustic holiday decor, golds, silvers, and plaids, while singing Christmas carols at the top of my lungs. We make peppermint-bark cookies, layered eggnog cake, and decorate log-cabin-style gingerbread houses. Crafted paper snowflakes hang from the fireplace and we giggle at our dog, Jackson, as he pulls off his reindeer antler headband. *Home Alone* plays on repeat as the younger boys write letters to Santa, still believing in the magic. I'll keep it alive as long as I can.

Christmas Tree Hunting

WHEN YOU LIVE in the Rocky Mountains of Wyoming, cutting down your own Christmas tree is a rite of passage.

I had never experienced a white Christmas. Growing up, when we shopped for a tree it was in the Home Depot parking lot. The trees were sprayed with fake snow, the weather was typically in the high 70s, and Santa was wearing a Hawaiian shirt and sunglasses. I had dreams of a white Christmas in the mountains, like you'd see in a Hallmark movie. I dreamed of creating new traditions with my family, like cutting down our own tree and decorating it together while drinking hot chocolate by a crackling fire.

When we moved to Jackson, I had my chance. I remember our first tree cutting like it was yesterday.

Have you seen National Lampoon's *Christmas Vacation*? It is arguably the best holiday movie ever made. Chevy Chase drags his unwilling family miles into the snow in search of the perfect Christmas tree. The daughter freezes from the waist down, the son is relentlessly complaining, the tree is three times too big, and their hands are covered in sap for days. And we mustn't forget the squirrel who hitched a ride home with the tree and destroyed their living room. Well, as it turns out, art imitates life. Our first Christmas tree hunt was an unintentional comedy act.

We had enough sense to keep the kids at home, there was no squirrel, and my living room is still intact. But freezing? Yes. Sap for days? Yes. Car stuck in the snow? Yes. Laughing so hard as we awkwardly tried to carry the *very* heavy tree back to the truck in knee deep snow, that I peed my pants? Yes. (Just a *little*. I've had three kids, it happens.) Flat tire on the way home, stranding us on a snow-covered road in the middle of nowhere? YES. Tree three times too large for our living room? Yes.

Cutting down a Christmas tree in the mountains of Wyoming is an adventure, a very challenging, comical, and priceless adventure. We've promised to repeat it every year. Our life is far from a picturesque Hallmark movie, and I'm okay with that. I'm learning I'd rather have the chaos and laughter along the way; it makes the traditions and memories that much brighter. I imagine anyone watching us that day would have been laughing right along with us. We were not impressive. And I'll be honest, our skills haven't improved much. But at the end of the day we have a beautiful Christmas tree we chopped down ourselves. We have happy, healthy kids to decorate it. And a fire is crackling, right now, as I'm pouring hot chocolate.

That's my kind of movie.

Homemade Hot Chocolate

SERVES 4

- 3 cups whole milk
- 1 cup heavy cream
- 8 ounces high-quality milk or dark chocolate, finely chopped
- ¼ cup granulated sugar
- 1 teaspoon vanilla bean paste or pure vanilla extract
- 1 teaspoon ground espresso powder (optional)

Pinch of kosher salt

Homemade Vanilla Marshmallows (page 133) or Vanilla Whipped Cream (page 124)

Pinch of cinnamon

In a medium saucepan over medium-low heat, combine the whole milk, cream, and chopped chocolate, whisking often until the chocolate has melted into the milk. Don't let it boil.

Whisk in the sugar. Allow to barely simmer, whisking occasionally.

Remove from the heat and whisk in the vanilla, espresso powder, if using, and salt. Pour into mugs and top with marshmallows or whipped cream and a sprinkle of cinnamon.

Bourbon Banana Cake with
Bourbon Cream Cheese Buttercream

MAKES 1 (4-LAYER 6-INCH) CAKE; MAKES ABOUT 1½ CUPS BOURBON BUTTERSCOTCH

FOR THE CAKE

- 3 cups all-purpose flour
- 1 teaspoon baking soda
- 1 teaspoon baking powder
- 1½ teaspoons ground cinnamon
- ¼ teaspoon freshly ground nutmeg
- ¾ teaspoon kosher salt
- ¾ cup unsalted butter, room temperature
- 1 cup granulated sugar
- ½ cup packed dark brown sugar
- 3 large eggs, room temperature
- 1 tablespoon pure vanilla extract
- 3 large, very ripe, bananas, fork-mashed
- 1¼ cups buttermilk, room temperature
- ¼ cup high-quality bourbon whiskey

BOURBON CREAM CHEESE BUTTERCREAM

- 1 cup unsalted butter, room temperature
- 1 (8-ounce) block full-fat cream cheese, room temperature
- 5½ cups confectioners' sugar, sifted
- 2 to 3 tablespoons bourbon whiskey
- Pinch of kosher salt

FOR THE BOURBON BUTTERSCOTCH

- ½ cup unsalted butter
- 1½ cups turbinado sugar
- ½ cup heavy cream, room temperature
- ½ cup bourbon whiskey
- 1½ teaspoons kosher salt
- 1 teaspoon pure vanilla bean paste

Preheat the oven to 350 degrees F. Butter 4 (6-inch) cake pans and line the bottoms with parchment paper. Dust the interior of the pans generously with flour, then tip over to knock out the excess, leaving a thin coating. Set aside.

To make the cake, in a medium bowl, whisk together the flour, baking soda, baking powder, cinnamon, nutmeg, and salt. Set aside.

In the bowl of an electric mixer on medium-high speed, beat the butter and sugars until light and fluffy, about 3 minutes.

With the mixer on low speed, add the eggs, 1 at a time, mixing well after

continued >

each addition. Stop to scrape down the bowl. Add the vanilla extract. Mix until combined.

Add the mashed bananas. Mix until combined. Scrape down the bowl.

With the mixer on low speed, add half of the dry ingredients, followed by half of the buttermilk. Mix for about 20 seconds, scraping down the bowl if needed. Repeat with the remaining dry ingredients, followed by the remaining buttermilk, scraping down the bowl as needed. With the mixer on low speed, slowly add the bourbon. Mix for about 30 seconds until combined. Do not overmix. Pour the batter evenly among the pans.

Bake on the center rack for about 25 to 27 minutes, or until a tester inserted into the center of the cakes comes out clean. Allow the cakes to cool in their pans for 10 minutes before turning over onto a wire rack. Allow them to cool completely before frosting.

To make the buttercream, in the bowl of an electric mixer on medium high speed, cream together the butter and the cream cheese until light and fluffy, about 3 minutes. Add the confectioners' sugar, 1 cup at a time, mixing for about 30 seconds after each addition. Add the bourbon to taste, and salt. Mix until combined. On medium speed, mix for 3 minutes until light and fluffy.

To make the butterscotch, in a medium saucepan over medium heat, melt the butter. Add the sugar and stir to combine. Raise the heat to medium-high and continue stirring for 1 minute. Carefully pour in the heavy cream, bourbon, and salt. Bring the mixture to a boil and stir constantly for 8 to 10 minutes until the mixture begins to come together and pulls away from the sides. Remove from the heat and stir in the vanilla bean paste. Pour the butterscotch into a heat-proof container and allow it to cool to room temperature.

The butterscotch thickens as it cools. If needed, reheat to bring it back to a pourable consistency.

To assemble the cake, place 1 cooled cake layer, flat side facing down, on a cake plate. Cover the top with a generous layer of bourbon buttercream. Add a spoonful of room temperature (not warm) butterscotch, leaving a 1-inch border around the cake edges. You don't want the butterscotch leaking out of the sides. Place the second cake layer, flat side facing up, on top of the frosted first layer. Fill the gaps between the cake layers with buttercream. Repeat the steps with the buttercream and butterscotch. Fill the gaps between the cake layers with buttercream. Place the final cake layer, flat side facing up. Cover the top and sides of the cake with a thin coat of buttercream to lock in the crumbs, scraping off the excess for a semi-naked finish. Refrigerate the cake for 20 minutes before adding a butterscotch drip.

To add a butterscotch drip, reheat the remaining butterscotch in the microwave for about 10 seconds. Stir. Allow the butterscotch to cool slightly, but make sure it's a pourable consistency. You want it slightly warmer than room temperature. Using a large spoon, pour the butterscotch over the top of the chilled cake, pushing it gently to the edges, allowing it to drip down over the sides.

NOTES: While frosting this cake, I left some of the cake layer exposed. I added dried greenery and edible gold leaf to the sides. My favorite bourbon whiskey is Wyoming Whiskey. Their small-batch bourbon whiskey has warm notes of vanilla, caramel, browned butter, and toffee, which make it a perfect addition to baked goods.

Peppermint Bark Chocolate Sandwich Cookies

MAKES 28 (3-INCH) COOKIE SANDWICHES

FOR THE COOKIES

- 1 cup unsalted butter, room temperature
- ¼ cup vegetable shortening
- 1½ cups granulated sugar
- 2 large eggs, room temperature
- 2 teaspoons pure vanilla extract
- 1 teaspoon pure peppermint extract
- ½ teaspoon kosher salt
- ¾ teaspoon baking powder
- ⅓ cup unsweetened Dutch-process cocoa powder
- ⅓ cup black cocoa powder
- 3 cups all-purpose flour, plus more if needed and for rolling

FOR THE WHITE CHOCOLATE BUTTERCREAM FILLING

- ½ cup unsalted butter, room temperature
- ⅓ cup white chocolate chips, melted and cooled to room temperature
- 1¾ cups confectioners' sugar, sifted
- 1 teaspoon pure vanilla extract
- 1 tablespoon heavy cream

Pinch of kosher salt
- ½ cup crushed candy canes for garnish
- ½ cup white chocolate chips, melted, for drizzling

To make the cookies, in the bowl of an electric mixer on medium-high speed, cream the butter, shortening, and sugar together until light and fluffy, about 2 minutes. Add the eggs, 1 at a time, mixing well after each addition. Add the vanilla extract and peppermint extract. Mix until fully combined. Scrape down the bowl as needed. Add the salt, baking powder, and cocoas. Mix until fully combined. Add the flour, 1 cup at a time, mixing after each addition, until the dough comes together. If the dough still seems sticky, add additional flour by the tablespoon. Cover the dough and refrigerate for at least 1 hour.

Preheat the oven to 375 degrees F. Line 2 baking sheets with parchment paper.

On a well-floured surface, roll the dough to ¼ inch thick. Use your favorite cookie cutters to cut into shapes and place on the prepared baking sheets, leaving an inch or so between cookies. Bake on the center rack for 8 to 10 minutes, until slightly crisp around the edges. Repeat with remaining dough. Allow the cookies to cool on a wire rack.

continued >

To make the filling, in the bowl of an electric mixer on high speed, cream the butter and melted white chocolate until light and fluffy, about 2 minutes. Add the confectioners' sugar. Mix to combine. Add the vanilla, cream, and salt. Mix on medium high speed for about 3 minutes, until fluffy and smooth.

Using a rubber spatula or wooden spoon, stir by hand to remove any air bubbles.

Spoon the filling into a pastry bag with the tip cut off. You can also use a butter knife or spoon for the filling if you like a more rustic look.

To assemble the cookies, swirl the filling over the top of one cookie and firmly press another cookie on top, being careful not to break it. Dip the sides of the cookies in crushed candy canes. Drizzle the tops with white chocolate. Refrigerate the cookies, covered, for about 30 minutes to firm up the filling.

Store the cookies in an airtight container; they can be kept refrigerated for 1 week.

Grand Marnier Million Dollar Shortbread Bars

MAKES 18 BARS

FOR THE ORANGE-ZESTED SHORTBREAD CRUST

- 2 cups plus 3 tablespoons all-purpose flour
- ½ cup granulated sugar
- ½ teaspoon kosher salt
- 1 cup unsalted butter, cold and cut into small cubes
- 1 teaspoon pure vanilla extract
- 1 tablespoon freshly grated orange zest

FOR THE GRAND MARNIER BUTTERSCOTCH FILLING

- ½ cup unsalted butter
- 1½ cups turbinado sugar
- ½ cup heavy cream, room temperature
- 1½ teaspoons kosher salt
- ⅓ cup Grand Marnier
- 1 teaspoon vanilla bean paste

FOR THE BITTERSWEET CHOCOLATE TOPPING

- 8 ounces high-quality bittersweet chocolate, chopped
- 2 tablespoons unsalted butter

continued >

Preheat the oven to 350 degrees F. Butter an 8 x 10-inch baking pan and line with parchment paper. Allow the parchment paper to hang over the edge of the pan so that you can pull the bars out easily after baking.

To make the crust, in a food processor, combine the flour, sugar, and salt. Pulse until combined. Add the cubed butter and vanilla extract. Pulse until the mixture resembles coarse crumbs. Add the orange zest. Pulse until just combined. Using your fingers or a rubber spatula, firmly press the dough into the prepared pan, spreading evenly to coat the bottom. Bake for 20 minutes, until lightly browned. Set aside to cool as you make the filling.

To make the filling, in a medium saucepan over medium heat, melt the butter. Add the sugar and stir to combine. Raise the heat to medium high and continue stirring for 1 minute. Carefully pour in the cream, salt, and Grand Marnier. Bring the mixture to a boil and stir constantly for 8 to 10 minutes until the mixture begins to come together and pulls

away from the sides. Remove from the heat and stir in the vanilla bean paste. Pour the butterscotch into a heatproof container and allow it to cool to room temperature.

The butterscotch thickens as it cools. If needed, reheat to bring back a pourable consistency.

Pour the butterscotch over the crust and spread to the edges in an even layer. Refrigerate for at least 1 hour and up to overnight until the butterscotch is firm.

To make the topping, in a medium saucepan over low heat, melt the chocolate and butter. Stir until smooth. Remove from the heat and allow to cool slightly.

Pour the chocolate over the butterscotch layer and spread to the edges in an even layer. Refrigerate the bars for 20 minutes until the chocolate is set.

Remove the bars from the pan and cut into rectangles. Store cookies in an airtight container for up to 1 week.

Death by Chocolate Cookies

MAKES 24 COOKIES

2 cups all-purpose flour

2 teaspoons cornstarch

⅔ cup good-quality Dutch-process dark cocoa powder, sifted

1 teaspoon espresso powder

1 teaspoon baking soda

1 teaspoon kosher salt

16 ounces bittersweet chocolate, chopped into chunks

1 cup unsalted butter, room temperature

1½ cups packed brown sugar

½ cup granulated sugar

4 large eggs, room temperature

1 tablespoon pure vanilla extract

1½ cups milk chocolate toffee bars, such as Heath, chopped into ½-inch chunks

8 ounces high-quality dark chocolate, chopped into chunks

Flaked sea salt

In a large bowl, sift together the flour, cornstarch, cocoa powder, espresso powder, baking soda, and salt. Set aside.

Place the bittersweet chocolate in a heatproof bowl set over a pot filled with 1 inch of simmering water. Make sure the water doesn't touch the bottom of the bowl. Stir until the chocolate is melted and smooth. Allow to cool to room temperature.

In the bowl of an electric mixer on medium speed, cream the butter and sugars until light and fluffy, about 3 minutes. On low speed, add the eggs, 1 at a time, mixing well after each addition. Add the vanilla extract. Scrape down the bowl as needed. On low speed, add the melted chocolate. Mix until combined. On low speed, add the flour mixture in 2 batches. Mix until just combined. Stir in the chopped toffee bars and dark chocolate chunks.

Cover and refrigerate for 1 hour.

Preheat the oven to 350 degrees F. Line 2 baking sheets with parchment paper.

Using a spoon or small ice-cream scoop, drop the batter on the baking sheets about 2 inches apart. Bake about 12 minutes, until just crisp on the edges.

Remove the cookies from the oven and sprinkle generously with flaked sea salt. Allow the cookies to cool on the baking sheet for 5 minutes, then transfer to a wire rack to cool. Store the cookies in an airtight container at room temperature for up to 5 days.

Brown Butter Chocolate Chip Cookies
with Espresso and Sea Salt

MAKES ABOUT 24 COOKIES

¾ cup unsalted butter

2¼ cups all-purpose flour

2 teaspoons cornstarch

1 teaspoon baking soda

½ teaspoon kosher or sea salt

¼ cup good-quality espresso powder

¾ cup packed brown sugar

½ cup granulated sugar

1 large egg, room temperature

1 large egg yolk, room temperature

1 tablespoon pure vanilla extract

8 ounces dark chocolate, chopped into chunks

Flaked sea salt

To brown the butter, in a medium skillet over medium heat, melt the butter, whisking constantly for 5 to 6 minutes. The butter will foam up and begin to smell nutty. It'll change to a light brown color and you'll see light brown colored specks at the bottom of the pan. Pour the butter in a heatproof bowl, making sure to get all the browned specks. Set aside and let it cool to room temperature.

In a large bowl, whisk together the flour, cornstarch, baking soda, salt, and espresso powder. Set aside.

In the bowl of an electric mixer on medium speed, mix the browned butter and sugars until no brown sugar lumps remain, about 2 minutes. Add the egg, egg yolk, and vanilla extract. Mix well. With the mixer on low speed, slowly add the dry ingredients. Mix until just combined. With a rubber spatula or wooden spoon, mix in the chocolate chunks.

Cover the cookie dough and refrigerate for at least two hours. Allow the dough to sit at room temperature for 30 minutes before baking.

Preheat the oven to 350 degrees F. Line 2 baking sheets with parchment paper.

Working with a generous spoonful of dough, roll into balls, and arrange them 3 inches apart on the baking sheet. Bake for 12 to 13 minutes, until the cookies are lightly browned on the edges. Sprinkle the cookies with flaked sea salt while they're still hot.

Allow the cookies to cool for 5 minutes on the baking sheet before transferring to a wire rack to cool completely.

Store cookies in an airtight container at room temperature for up to 1 week.

BAKING WITH KIDS

I REMEMBER ONE particular Sunday morning when we were making rolled sugar cookies . . .

"Momma, I can help you?" says my two-year-old, in his irresistible broken toddler speech. His hands still sticky from breakfast, his glossy brown eyes as big as gum balls, that one perfect curl resting on his forehead. He reaches up toward the counter and knocks the measured cup of sugar onto the floor; it spreads everywhere, covering the tile like snow. Unfazed, he reaches for the eggs, his tiny fingers grabbing one, along with the wooden spoon. He runs off into the family room, egg and spoon in hand, proudly shouting, "I helping, I helping!" I hear a thump and the crack of an eggshell on the floor, then "Uh oh . . ." I take a deep breath, grab the mop, and remind myself: good moms have sticky floors, dirty ovens, and happy kids.

I believe this to be true, but this practice isn't easy for me. I am a perfectionist to the core, especially in the kitchen. The kitchen is the one place in my home where I have a fragment of order. It's my happy place; it's where I create and work. But when little, my boys were constantly in the kitchen, creating tornados of madness, using spatulas for sword fights, chasing the cat into the dishwasher, destroying whatever I was working on. I sent them to the playroom, to their bedrooms, outside, but they would always find their way back to the kitchen. Not because it's their happy place, but because I'm their happy place.

My little boys didn't need clean counters or organized cabinets. They weren't bothered by sticky floors, dirty dishes, and broken egg shells. They didn't care if their cookies were picture perfect. They just wanted to share in what I was doing. They wanted to explore, to create. I could have driven myself insane trying to control every little mess, or I could relax and embrace having boys who wanted to learn and spend time with their mom. I chose sticky floors, dirty ovens, and happy kids.

Happiness is simple; it's in being together. These moments with my boys are fleeting and so precious. A moment ago they were toddlers, now they're on their way to being grown and heading out the door. When they look back, they won't remember the perfect kitchen; they'll remember the baking, the learning, and the laughter.

So when they were little, I let them get sticky, I let them paint with flour on the floor, I let them play with the cookie dough. And whenever they still want to, I let them mound frosting and sprinkles high. I share with them my love for baking and they share with me their joy. It's not messes we're creating, but memories.

Bake with your kids. It's a wonderful craft that teaches motor skills, math, measuring, artistic expression, and patience and they'll be so proud of what they create. Time in the kitchen is quality time. Embrace the moment; cleaning up can wait.

Rolled Sugar Cookies

MAKES 24 (3-INCH) COOKIES

2¾ cups all-purpose flour plus extra for rolling out the dough
⅓ cup cornstarch
¾ teaspoon kosher salt
1 cup unsalted butter, room temperature
4 ounces full-fat cream cheese
1 cup granulated sugar
1 large egg, room temperature
1 tablespoon pure vanilla extract

In a medium bowl, whisk together the flour, cornstarch, and salt. Set aside. In the bowl of an electric mixer on high speed, cream the butter, cream cheese, and sugar together until combined, about 2 minutes. Add the egg and vanilla. Mix until fully combined, scraping down the bowl as needed. With the mixer on low speed, add the flour mixture. Continue mixing on medium-low speed until the dough comes together. Wrap the dough in plastic wrap and refrigerate for 30 minutes to an hour.

Preheat the oven to 375 degrees F. Line 2 baking sheets with parchment paper.

On a well-floured surface, roll the dough to ¼ inch thick. Use your favorite cookie cutters to cut into shapes and place on the prepared baking sheets, leaving an inch or so between cookies. Bake on the center rack for 11 to 12 minutes. Repeat with remaining dough. Allow the cookies to cool on a wire rack. Decorate as desired.

These cookies will keep in an airtight container at room temperature for 2 weeks.

Gingerbread Sugar Cookies

MAKES 30 (3-INCH) COOKIES

1 cup unsalted butter, room temperature

1½ cups packed dark brown sugar

⅓ cup blackstrap molasses

2 large eggs, room temperature

⅓ cup cornstarch

1 tablespoon ground cinnamon

½ teaspoon ground allspice

2 teaspoons ground ginger

⅛ teaspoon ground cloves

¾ teaspoon kosher salt

4 to 4½ cups all-purpose flour plus extra flour for rolling

Vanilla Royal Icing (page 194)

Preheat the oven to 375 degrees F. Line 2 baking sheets with parchment paper and set aside.

In the bowl of an electric mixer on medium-high speed, cream the butter and brown sugar together until light and fluffy, about 2 minutes. Add the molasses. Mix until combined. Add the eggs, 1 at a time, mixing well after each addition. Scrape down the bowl as needed. With the mixer on low speed, add the cornstarch, cinnamon, allspice, ginger, cloves, and salt. Mix until combined. With the mixer on low speed, add 2 cups of flour. Mix until combined. Add the remaining flour, ½ cup at a time, until you reach 4 cups. If the dough starts to come together and pulls away from the sides of the bowl, stop adding flour. If needed, add the additional half cup of flour.

On a well-floured surface, roll the dough out to about ⅜ inch thick (the thicker the cookie, the chewier it will be). Use your favorite cookie cutters to cut into shapes. Transfer to the prepared baking sheets.

Bake on the center rack for 12 to 14 minutes, until the cookies look crisp on the edges and slightly soft in the center. Allow the cookies to cool for 5 minutes on the baking sheets and then transfer to a wire rack to cool completely. Decorate using royal icing as desired. These cookies will keep in an airtight container at room temperature for up to 2 weeks.

continued >

Vanilla Royal Icing

MAKES ABOUT 5 CUPS

⅓ cup meringue powder
⅔ cup warm water
1 (2-pound) bag confectioners' sugar
1 tablespoon pure vanilla extract
Pinch of kosher salt

In the bowl of an electric mixer using the whisk attachment on medium high speed, whisk together the meringue powder and warm water until light and frothy, about 3 minutes. Scrape down the sides of the bowl as needed. Add the confectioners' sugar. Mix on medium speed until the sugar is combined. Then mix on high speed for an additional 2 minutes. Add the vanilla extract and salt and mix to combine.

Transfer the icing to an airtight container. If you're not using the icing to decorate immediately, cover the top of the icing with a damp paper towel to prevent a crust from forming. The icing will keep for 2 weeks in the refrigerator.

NOTES: To decorate the cookies on the previous page with snowflakes I used Wilton tips 1, 2, and 3. The royal icing was medium consistency, which is slightly thinner than the consistency of toothpaste.

Spiced-Eggnog Cake

MAKES 1 (10-CUP) BUNDT CAKE; MAKES 2 CUPS GLAZE

FOR THE CAKE

- 1 tablespoon unsalted butter, melted
- 3 cups all-purpose flour plus extra for flouring the pan
- 1 teaspoon baking powder
- ½ teaspoon baking soda
- 1 teaspoon kosher salt
- 1¼ teaspoons freshly ground nutmeg, divided
- 1 tablespoon freshly grated orange zest
- ¾ cup eggnog, room temperature
- 1 tablespoon pure vanilla extract
- 4 tablespoons dark spiced rum, divided
- 1 cup plus 2 tablespoons unsalted butter, room temperature
- 1½ cups granulated sugar
- ½ cup packed light brown sugar
- 4 large eggs, room temperature
- ½ teaspoon ground cinnamon
- ¼ teaspoon ground allspice

FOR THE SPICED-EGGNOG GLAZE

- 3 tablespoons butter, melted and slightly cooled
- 2 ounces full-fat cream cheese, room temperature
- 3 cups confectioners' sugar, sifted
- ¼ cup eggnog

- 3 tablespoons spiced dark rum
- 1 teaspoon pure vanilla extract
- ¼ teaspoon freshly ground nutmeg
- Pinch of kosher salt

Preheat the oven to 350 degrees F. Using a pastry brush, generously brush the interior of a 10-cup Bundt cake pan with the melted butter, making sure to coat all the corners. Dust the interior with flour and then turn it over to shake out the excess. Set aside.

To make the cake, in a medium bowl, whisk together the flour, baking powder, baking soda, salt, ¼ teaspoon nutmeg, and orange zest. Set aside. In another medium bowl, whisk together the eggnog, vanilla extract, and 2 tablespoons rum. Set aside.

In the bowl of an electric mixer on medium-high speed, combine the butter and sugars, and then beat until light and fluffy, about 3 minutes. Scrape down the bowl. Add the eggs, 1 at a time, mixing well after each addition. Scrape down the bowl. With the mixer on low speed, add ½ of the flour mixture. Mix for 20 seconds. Follow with half of the

continued ›

eggnog mixture. Repeat. Scrape down the bowl as needed.

In a separate bowl, mix 1½ cups of the cake batter with the remaining 2 tablespoons spiced rum, the remaining 1 teaspoon ground nutmeg, cinnamon, and allspice. Stir until combined.

Pour half of the main batter in the bottom of the cake pan. Then pour the spiced batter over the top. To create a marbled effect, using a butter knife or rubber spatula, mix the spiced batter into the main batter, using a zigzag pattern. Do not over mix. Pour the remaining batter over the top.

Bake on the center rack for 55 to 60 minutes, or until a tester inserted into the center of the cake comes out clean. Allow the cake to cool in the pan on a wire rack for 25 to 30 minutes. Turn the cake over, carefully releasing it from the pan onto the wire rack. Allow the cake to continue cooling while you make the glaze.

To make the glaze, in the bowl of an electric mixer on medium speed, combine the melted butter and cream cheese. Add half the confectioners' sugar, followed by half of the eggnog, mixing well after each addition. Add the remaining confectioners' sugar, followed by the remaining eggnog. Add the rum, vanilla extract, nutmeg, and salt. Mix on medium speed for 2 minutes until silky smooth. If the glaze is too thick, add a touch more eggnog and mix to combine.

Using a spoon, generously drizzle the glaze over the cake while it's still slightly warm. Let the cake stand for 30 minutes to set the glaze. Serve at room temperature.

NOTES: I decorated this cake with sprigs of fresh rosemary and fresh cranberries coated in edible gold luster dust.

Bailey's Mocha Cake

MAKES 1 (3-LAYER 8-INCH) CAKE

FOR THE CAKE

   2 cups all-purpose flour
1¾ cups granulated sugar
   ¾ cup Dutch-processed cocoa powder, sifted
   2 teaspoons baking soda
   1 teaspoon baking powder
   1 teaspoon kosher salt
   2 teaspoons ground espresso powder
   2 large eggs, room temperature
   ½ cup canola oil or vegetable oil
   1 cup buttermilk, room temperature
   1 tablespoon pure vanilla extract
   1 cup freshly brewed hot coffee

FOR THE WHIPPED COFFEE GANACHE

1½ cups heavy cream
1¼ cups finely chopped high quality dark or bittersweet chocolate
1½ teaspoons ground espresso powder
   1 teaspoon vanilla extract
Pinch of kosher salt

FOR THE BAILEY'S BUTTERCREAM

   2 cups unsalted butter, room temperature
   6 cups confectioners' sugar, sifted
   ⅓ cup Bailey's Original Irish Cream
   ¼ teaspoon ground cinnamon
   ⅛ teaspoon kosher salt

Preheat the oven to 350 degrees F. Butter 3 (8-inch) cake pans and line the bottoms with parchment paper. Dust the interior of the pans generously with cocoa powder, then tip over to knock out the excess, leaving a thin coating. Set aside.

To make the cake, in the bowl of an electric mixer on low speed, mix the flour, sugar, cocoa powder, baking soda, baking powder, salt, and espresso powder until well combined.

In a medium bowl, whisk the eggs, oil, buttermilk, and vanilla extract until well combined. Very slowly, while whisking, add the hot coffee to the buttermilk mixture.

With the mixer on low speed, add the buttermilk mixture to the cocoa mixture. Stop to scrape down the sides and bottom of the bowl, then mix on medium speed for 45 to 60 seconds until fully combined. The batter will be very thin.

Pour the batter evenly among the pans. Bake on the center rack for about 25 to 27 minutes, or until a tester inserted into

continued >

the center of the cakes comes out clean. Allow the cakes to cool in the pans for 10 minutes before turning over onto a wire rack. Allow them to cool completely before frosting.

To make the ganache, in a double boiler over medium heat, combine the cream, chocolate, and espresso powder. Stir often, until melted and smooth. Remove from the heat and stir in the vanilla extract and salt.

Cover and refrigerate for 4 hours or overnight until thickened.

When ready to use, transfer the ganache to the bowl of an electric mixer. Beat the ganache on medium-high speed until stiff, but still spreadable, 30 to 60 seconds.

To make the buttercream, in the bowl of an electric mixer on medium high speed, cream the butter and until light and fluffy, about 3 minutes. Add the confectioners' sugar, 1 cup at a time, mixing for about 30 seconds after each addition. Add the Bailey's, cinnamon, and salt. Mix until combined. On medium speed, mix for 3 minutes until light and fluffy.

To assemble the cake, place 1 cooled cake layer, flat side facing down, on a cake plate. Cover the top with a generous layer of Bailey's buttercream. Add a generous spoonful of the coffee ganache, leaving a 1-inch border around the cake edges. You don't want the ganache leaking out of the sides. Place the second cake layer, flat side facing up, on top of the frosted first layer. Fill the gaps between the cake layers with buttercream. Repeat the steps with the buttercream and ganache. Fill the gaps between the cake layers with buttercream. Place the final cake layer, flat side facing up. Cover the top and sides of the cake with a thin coat of buttercream to lock in the crumbs. Refrigerate for 15 minutes, uncovered. Remove the cake from the fridge and, with an offset spatula, apply a generous layer of buttercream frosting over the entire cake, starting at the top and smoothing down and over the sides.

NOTES: I decorated this cake with a palette knife and painting technique. The buttercream colors were tinted with Colour Mill oil-based food gels in Olive, Forest, Chocolate, Mustard, Concrete, Lemon, and Clay.

Brown Butter and Bourbon Pecan Pie with Bittersweet Chocolate

MAKES 1 (9-INCH) SINGLE-CRUST PIE; MAKES 1 CUP WHIPPED CREAM

FOR THE FLAKY BUTTER CRUST

- 1¼ cups all-purpose flour
- ½ tablespoon granulated sugar
- ½ teaspoon fine sea salt
- 8 tablespoons unsalted butter, well chilled and cut into cubes
- ½ tablespoon apple cider vinegar
- ¼ cup ice water, plus a few table-spoons more if needed

Heavy cream for brushing

Coarse sugar for sprinkling

PECAN FILLING

- ½ cup unsalted butter, browned (see page 76) and cooled to room temperature
- 3 large eggs, room temperature
- 1 cup packed dark brown sugar
- ½ cup honey
- ½ cup molasses
- 3 tablespoons bourbon whiskey
- 2 tablespoons pure vanilla extract
- ¼ teaspoon ground nutmeg
- ¼ teaspoon ground cinnamon
- 2 cups pecans, chopped, plus 1 cup whole pecans for decorating
- 1 cup chopped high-quality bitter-sweet chocolate

BOURBON VANILLA WHIPPED CREAM

- 1 cup heavy cream, very cold
- 1 tablespoon granulated sugar
- 1 tablespoon bourbon whiskey
- 1 teaspoon vanilla bean paste

To make the crust, in a large bowl, mix the flour, sugar, and sea salt. Add the cubed butter. With a pastry blender, blend until the mixture begins to resemble small peas.

Mix the vinegar into the ice water. Drizzle a few tablespoons of water over the flour and butter mixture and mix with a fork. Add more water until the dough begins to come together. Once the dough becomes moist and clumps together, it's hydrated enough.

Gather the dough into a ball. Flatten it into a disk and wrap in plastic wrap. Refrigerate for 1 hour. Remove the dough 30 minutes before you're ready to use so it will roll out easily.

Th dough will keep in the fridge, tightly wrapped in plastic, for 1 week, and will keep frozen for 1 month.

Roll out one disk of dough on a well-floured surface to a 12-inch circle. The dough should be larger than the 9-inch pie dish.

Carefully transfer the dough to the pie dish. I fold the dough over my rolling pin to make it easy. Gently press the dough into the sides of the dish, leaving about an inch of overhang on the sides. Fold the overhanging dough over the top and crimp the sides together. You can add a decorative braid for a festive touch. Refrigerate while you prepare the filling.

Preheat the oven to 425 degrees F.

To make the filling, in a large bowl, combine the cooled brown butter, eggs, brown sugar, honey, molasses, bourbon, vanilla extract, nutmeg, and cinnamon. Whisk together until smooth. Gently fold in the chopped pecans and chopped bittersweet chocolate.

Pour the filling into the prepared pie crust. Place the whole pecans in a decorative pattern on the top of the pie. Brush the pie crust edges with heavy cream and sprinkle generously with sugar. Bake the pie on the center rack for 10 minutes, then reduce the oven temperature to 375 degrees F. Bake for an additional 40 to 45 minutes until the crust is golden brown and the center of the pie jiggles slightly.

Transfer to a wire rack to cool for 1 hour. Then refrigerate the pie for at least 4 hours, until the center is set completely. This pie can be made 3 days ahead, kept covered, and refrigerated. Serve with Bourbon Vanilla Whipped Cream.

To make the whipped cream, for best results, chill the metal bowl of your electric mixer for 20 minutes ahead of time. Using the whisk attachment, add the cream to the chilled bowl. Beat on medium-high speed until soft peaks form. Add the sugar, bourbon, and vanilla bean paste. Continue beating for 20 to 30 seconds more until stiff peaks form. Be careful to not over beat. Serve immediately.

Mint Chip Cupcakes

MAKES 12 CUPCAKES

FOR THE CUPCAKES

- 1 cup all-purpose flour
- ½ teaspoon baking soda
- ½ teaspoon kosher salt
- ½ cup boiling water
- ½ cup Dutch-processed cocoa powder
- 2 ounces high-quality dark chocolate, chopped
- 2 teaspoons ground espresso powder
- ¾ cup granulated sugar
- ½ cup sour cream, room temperature
- ½ cup canola or vegetable oil
- 2 large eggs, room temperature
- 2 teaspoons pure vanilla extract

FOR THE MINT CHIP BUTTERCREAM

- 1 cup unsalted butter, room temperature
- 3 cups confectioners' sugar
- ¼ cup heavy cream
- ½ teaspoon peppermint extract

Pinch of kosher salt

- 2 ounces high-quality dark chocolate, finely grated

Preheat the oven to 350 degrees F. Prepare the cupcake pan with paper liners. Set aside.

To make the cupcakes, in a medium bowl, whisk together the flour, baking soda, and salt. Set aside. In a large bowl, whisk together the boiling water, cocoa powder, dark chocolate, and espresso powder until smooth. Add the sugar, sour cream, oil, eggs, and vanilla extract. Whisk until smooth and fully combined. Add the dry ingredients and stir to just combine, making sure no flour lumps are left, but not overmixed.

Using an ice cream scoop or large spoon, fill each cupcake liner ⅔ full. Bake for 18 to 20 minutes, or until a tester inserted into the center of the cupcakes comes out clean. Allow the cupcakes to cool in the pan for 5 minutes, then transfer to a wire rack to cool completely.

continued >

To make the buttercream, in the bowl of an electric mixer on medium-high speed, cream the butter and until light

and fluffy, about 3 minutes. Add the confectioners' sugar, 1 cup at a time, mixing for about 30 seconds after each addition. Add the cream, peppermint extract, and salt. Mix until combined. On medium speed, mix for 3 minutes until light and fluffy. With a rubber spatula, stir in the grated chocolate.

Top each cupcake with a generous swirl of Mint Chip Buttercream.

NOTES: To create the topper for these cupcakes, I melted dark chocolate and spread it over a piece of crumpled aluminum foil. I let the chocolate set and peeled the foil off. I dusted the chocolate with green shimmer luster dust. Then I broke the chocolate into pieces. Buttercream swirl is made with Ateco tip 829.

Prosecco Rose Cupcakes

MAKES 12 CUPCAKES

FOR THE PROSECCO REDUCTION
- 1 cup Prosecco

FOR THE CUPCAKES
- 1½ cups cake flour
- 1½ teaspoons baking powder
- ½ teaspoon kosher salt
- ⅓ cup whole milk, room temperature
- ½ teaspoon rosewater extract
- ½ cup unsalted butter, room temperature
- 1 cup granulated sugar
- 2 large eggs, room temperature
- 3 tablespoons Prosecco reduction

FOR THE ROSEWATER BUTTERCREAM
- 1 cup unsalted butter, room temperature
- 3 cups confectioners' sugar
- 2 tablespoons Prosecco reduction
- ¼ teaspoon rosewater extract

Pinch of kosher salt

Preheat the oven to 350 degrees F. Prepare the cupcake pans with paper liners. Set aside.

continued >

To make the Prosecco reduction, in a medium saucepan over medium-high heat, bring the Prosecco to a boil. Reduce the heat to low and simmer for 15 to 20 minutes, until the Prosecco has reduced to half. Set aside and allow to cool to room temperature.

To make the cake, in a medium bowl, whisk together the cake flour, baking powder, and salt. Set aside. In a medium measuring cup, combine the whole milk and rosewater extract. Set aside.

In the bowl of an electric mixer on medium-high speed, cream the butter and sugar together until light and fluffy, 3 minutes. On low speed, add the eggs, 1 at a time, mixing well after each addition. Scrape down the bowl as needed. On low speed, add half of the dry ingredients. Mix to combine. Then add half of the milk mixture. Mix to combine. Scrape down the bowl as needed. Repeat with the remaining dry ingredients and milk mixture. Mix for 20 seconds, until fully combined and smooth. Using a rubber spatula, stir in the Prosecco reduction until combined.

Using an ice cream scoop or large spoon, fill each cupcake liner ⅔ full. Bake for 18 to 19 minutes, or until a tester inserted into the center of the cupcakes comes out clean. Allow the cupcakes to cool in the pan for 5 minutes then transfer to a wire rack to cool completely.

To make the buttercream, in the bowl of an electric mixer on high speed, cream the butter until light and smooth, about 5 minutes. Add the confectioners' sugar, 1 cup at a time, mixing well after each addition. Scrape down the bowl. Add the Prosecco reduction, rosewater extract, and salt. Mix on medium-high speed for about 3 minutes, until fluffy and smooth. Using a rubber spatula or wooden spoon, stir to remove any air bubbles.

Top each cupcake with a generous swirl of Rosewater Buttercream.

NOTES: To make buttercream roses and leaves, I used Ateco piping tips 124K, 125K, and 126K. The buttercream was tinted with Colour Mill in Blush, Nude, and Olive.

White Chocolate Cranberry-Pistachio Bars

MAKES 18 BARS

FOR THE SUGAR COOKIE CRUST

1½ cups all-purpose flour
1 teaspoon cornstarch
¾ teaspoon kosher salt
10 tablespoons unsalted butter, room temperature
⅓ cup packed brown sugar
⅓ cup confectioners' sugar
1 egg yolk, room temperature
1 teaspoon pure vanilla extract

FOR THE WHITE CHOCOLATE FILLING

10 ounces high-quality white chocolate, chopped
1 cup dried cranberries
1 cup salted shelled pistachios, roughly chopped

Preheat the oven to 350 degrees F. Butter an 8 x 10-inch baking pan and line with parchment paper. Allow the parchment paper to hang over the edge of the pan so that you can pull the bars out easily after baking.

To make the crust, in a medium bowl, whisk together the flour, cornstarch, and salt. Set aside.

In the bowl of an electric mixer on medium-high speed, beat the butter and the sugars together until combined. Add the egg yolk and vanilla extract. Mix to combine. With the mixer on low speed, add the dry ingredients. Mix until just combined. Using your fingers or a rubber spatula, firmly press the dough into the prepared pan, spreading evenly to coat the bottom. Bake for 20 minutes, until lightly browned. Set aside to cool as you make the filling.

To make the filling, in a medium saucepan over low heat, melt the white chocolate. Stir until smooth. Remove from heat and allow to cool slightly.

Pour the white chocolate over the cooled sugar cookie crust. Using an angled spatula, spread the white chocolate in an even layer to the edges. Sprinkle the top with dried cranberries and pistachios. Refrigerate for 30 minutes until the chocolate is set. Lift the bars from the pan and cut into squares. Serve at room temperature.

Store the cookies in an airtight container at room temperature for up to 1 week.

ACKNOWLEDGMENTS

I HAVE WANTED TO MAKE THIS BOOK since I painted my first mountain scene on a buttercream cake. Much like a cake, this book came together in layers, supported by the wonderful people around me. I could not have done it without their encouragement, help, and dedication. I'm forever grateful.

My parents provided the all-important foundation layer. My mom has always been my biggest cheerleader, the voice in my head telling me to shine. Thank you for the unconditional love, for always being there to listen, for letting me eat all the chocolate chip cookie dough when I was little, for making homemade pies with me, and for teaching me the joy of baking. My father taught me to understand the value of hard work, discipline, and perseverance. Thank you, Dad, for giving me the tools I need to succeed, for always letting me know how proud you are, for helping me whenever I needed it, and for introducing us all to the beauty and peace of mountain life.

To my family and friends: You have shaped who I am. Thank you for all the years of lifting me up, being excited about what I do, believing in me, and for sending love and support even when you're miles away. I feel it.

To my cake community: I have made so many wonderful friends through Instagram, most of whom I've never met, but with whom I have a genuine bond. The support, encouragement, and camaraderie of this far-flung band of bakers has made me a better artist and baker and I am so appreciative of our open sharing of knowledge, ideas, and enthusiasm.

I am ever grateful to the event planners and clients of Jackson Hole, Wyoming. The experiences I've had, the projects I've been trusted with, the weddings I've witnessed—all I can say is, what a gift. Thank you for choosing me. You are the foundation of my career. It is an honor and a privilege to help you celebrate life's most beautiful moments.

After many years of perfecting my art, it's been my dream to create a book and share my knowledge and skills with others. Thank you, Chase Reynolds Ewald, for discovering me and for believing I had a talent worth sharing. Without you this book would not exist. Thank you for your guidance, your never-ending faith, your mentoring, and for being the best creative partner I could ever hope for. You made my dreams come true.

My editor, Michelle Branson, and the Gibbs Smith team, have made the process supportive and seamless. Thank you for providing an environment of creative freedom and for developing my ideas and skills into something real. As a first-time author and photographer, you made this process so enjoyable. Ryan Thomann had a vision for this book; designer Eva Spring and production designer Renee Bond turned it into something more beautiful than I ever dreamed.

Beth Behrs and Michael Gladdis trusted me with their most special day and allowed me to be a part of their wedding celebration, which was such an honor. Thank you, Beth, for reliving that day in your beautiful foreword to this book. I'm grateful to share a love of the Wild West with you, to have bonded through a love of baking, and to be privileged to call you a friend.

I can't do what I do without the solid grounding in home. My husband Jeremiah is truly my rock. Thank you, Jeremiah, for encouraging my wild ideas, comforting my doubts and fears, tasting endless batches of cake, helping me believe I could, and for building me a home bakery where I can practice my craft every day. Your faith in me, your sense of humor, and your adorable dimples carried me through.

To my boys, Hatton, Killian, and Soren, my sweet cookie eaters and cuddlebugs. Thank you for making me a mom and bringing joy and love into my life that words can never describe. You have given me the ability to see the world through a child's eyes and there is nothing more inspiring. All of this is for you.

INDEX

Metric Conversion Chart

VOLUME MEASUREMENTS		WEIGHT MEASUREMENTS		TEMPERATURE CONVERSION	
U.S.	METRIC	U.S.	METRIC	FAHRENHEIT	CELSIUS
1 teaspoon	5 ml	½ ounce	15 g	250	120
1 tablespoon	15 ml	1 ounce	30 g	300	150
¼ cup	60 ml	3 ounces	90 g	325	160
⅓ cup	75 ml	4 ounces	115 g	350	180
½ cup	125 ml	8 ounces	225 g	375	190
⅔ cup	150 ml	12 ounces	350 g	400	200
¾ cup	175 ml	1 pound	450 g	425	220
1 cup	250 ml	2¼ pounds	1 kg	450	230

ABOUT THE AUTHORS

LINDSEY JOHNSON is an artist, interior designer, content creator, baker, photographer, and foodie. She's also the mother of three boys and the keeper of chickens, pigs, goats, a dog, and a gentle Jersey cow named Trouble.

From her childhood in southern California to her Bachelor of Arts degree from the Interior Design Institute in Newport Beach, California, Lindsey has been a lifelong student of the arts. She designed interiors in custom residential homes in Newport Beach and Laguna Beach for a decade before she and her husband decided to relocate their young family to Wyoming. There, Lindsey nurtured her passion for baking by pursuing a professional career in artisan cakes, confections, food styling, and photography. She has discovered that her favorite artistic medium is butter and sugar and that she's never happier than when thinking about cake design, dinner-party settings, dessert-table styling, and making edible art to bring people joy. Known for her inventive wedding cakes and artful baked goods, Lindsey's work has been featured in *Brides*, *Martha Stewart Weddings*, *Carats & Cake*, and *Rocky Mountain Bride*.

Lindsey lives with her husband and three boys on a 20-acre ranch in Freedom, Wyoming, where the monumental landscape, wildlife migrations, and ever-changing seasons continue to provide endless inspiration for her art.

CHASE REYNOLDS EWALD'S career encompasses sixteen books, two Western Design Conference Sourcebooks, and hundreds of magazine articles. A graduate of Yale and U.C. Berkeley's Graduate School of Journalism, she is a freelance writer and editor who helps private clients craft their stories. Recent books include *By Western Hands: Functional Art from the Heart of the West* and *Rancho Sisquoc*. Chase collaborated with writer Heather Sandy Hebert on *Design Mixology: The Interiors of Tineke Triggs* and *At Home in the Wine Country*. She worked with photographer Audrey Hall to produce *Cabin Style*, *Rustic Modern*, *American Rustic*, *New West Cuisine*, *The New Western Home*, and the multi-award-winning *Bison: Portrait of an Icon*. An enthusiastic cook and road-tripper around the West, Chase lives in northern California with her husband, Charles, and their four daughters.